The Abiding Room

The Abiding Room™

*Experiencing the Abiding,
Spirit-Filled Life*

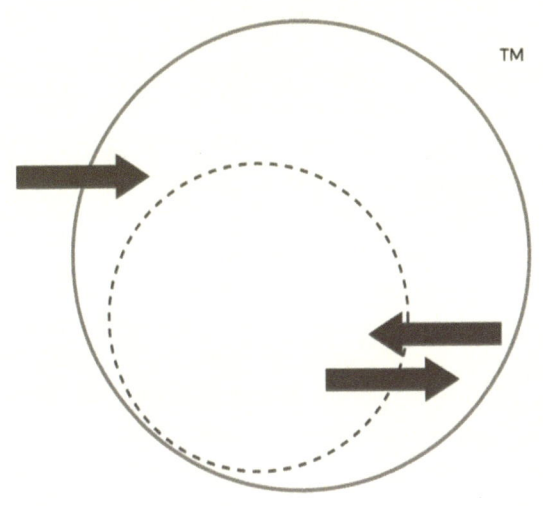

Questions Included for
Individual Reflection / Small Group Discussion

KEVIN SEACAT

The Abiding Room™

Copyright © 2025 by Kevin D. Seacat

Unless otherwise indicated, all Scripture quotations are from The Holy Bible, English Standard Version® (ESV*)* copyright © 2001 by Crossway, a publishing ministry of Good News Publishers. Used by permission. All rights reserved.

Scripture quotations marked (NIV) are taken from the Holy Bible, New International Version®. Copyright © 1973, 1978, 1984, 2011 by Biblica, Inc.™ Used by permission of Zondervan. All rights reserved worldwide. www.zondervan.com. The "NIV" and "New International Version" are trademarks registered in the United States Patent and Trademark Office by Biblica, Inc.™

Scripture quotations marked (NASB) are taken from the New American Standard Bible®, Copyright © 1960, 1962, 1968, 1971, 1972, 1973, 1975, 1977, 1995 by The Lockman Foundation. Used by permission.

Scripture quotations from *The Message*. Copyright © by Eugene Peterson 1993, 1994, 1995, 1996, 2000, 2001, 2002. Used by permission of Tyndale House Publishers, Inc.

Bolded words included in Scripture quotations have been added by the author for emphasis.

Any internet addresses (websites, etc.) in this book are offered as a resource. The author does not vouch for the content of these sites for the life of this book.

Friends of *The Abiding Room* are given permission to share, without alteration or resale, the contents of this book, or The Abiding Room website, in part or in full, royalty free.

For more information, or to contact the author, please email: TheAbidingRoom@gmail.com.

ISBN 979-8-9913609-2-0 (hardcover)
ISBN 979-8-9913609-3-7 (softcover)
ISBN 979-8-9913609-1-3 (eBook)
ISBN 979-8-9913609-0-6 (audio)

Cover design: Terry Dugan
Cover photo: Ilona@Adobe Stock
Artwork: Kara Rozendaal
Editorial team: Sheryl Moon, Jean Bloom, and Cristina Wright
Interior design: Katherine Lloyd, The DESK
Publishing services provided by BelieversBookServices.com

First printing: 2025

Printed in the United States of America

To my wife, Juli; my parents,
Dale and Bert; and my brother, Kent

The four of you made it easy to see that
God's love is unconditional,
because your love always is as well

Contents

Acknowledgments ix
Welcome to *The Abiding Room* xi

Part One: THE 3 LEVELS OF LIFE

Chapter 1   The 3 Levels of Life in the Old Testament 3
Chapter 2   The 3 Levels of Life in the New Testament 19

Part Two: THE HOLY SPIRIT

Chapter 3   The Battle of the Spirit and the Flesh 33
Chapter 4   Experiencing the Holy Spirit's Joy and Peace 45
Chapter 5   The Power of the Holy Spirit 57
Chapter 6   Be Filled with the Spirit 71

Part Three: THE ABIDING LIFE

Chapter 7   The Great 2 for 1 85
Chapter 8   The Vine and the Branches 93
Chapter 9   The Abiding Friendship 105

Part Four: SURRENDER

Chapter 10   Surrender Your Will 121
Chapter 11   Surrender Your Self-Effort 133
Chapter 12   Surrender Your Worldliness 147

Part Five: HOLY LIVING

Chapter 13   God Is Holy 163
Chapter 14   Repentance 177
Chapter 15   Forgiveness 191

Part Six: HOPE FOR THE WORLD

Chapter 16	Faith	207
Chapter 17	Church Unity and Revival	219
Chapter 18	A Call to Action	233
Appendix 1	The Good News	241
Appendix 2	Recommended Reading List	243
Appendix 3	Compilation of Abiding Truths	245
Appendix 4	Compilation of Suggested Songs	249
Appendix 5	Suggested 12–Week Group Schedule	253
	Notes	255
	About the Author	257

Acknowledgments

I am deeply grateful for the following people who God brought along at exactly the right time to help with this book:

Kara Rozendaal has worked with me since 1989. She is like the little sister I never had. Her tireless and patient constructions and reconstructions of PowerPoint slides and presentations since 2001 have been essential, and her friendship and the laughs we shared along the way have made the work a pleasure. Without her, the Abiding Room teaching would not exist.

Russ Heptinstall recorded video and spent hundreds of hours editing the first Abiding Room classes in 2004, the transcripts of which became the initial text of this book. He did early review and edits on the manuscript, and authored the reflection questions at the end of each chapter. In addition, his wife Jen was a great encouragement in the first classes and a great help in choosing the Suggested Songs.

My dear daughter Rachel was the first to see each chapter. Her suggestions and editing dramatically improved the content of this book. And my other dear daughter Abby joined in later and offered essential insights.

Sheryl Moon patiently guided me through multiple stages of greatly needed editing. The fingerprints of her wisdom and expertise are on every page of this book. Jean Bloom's editing smoothed and polished my mechanical writing style.

Ethan Pope, DJ Mullaney, Greg Parker, and Al Fadi reviewed the manuscript and made important contributions.

Dr. Darryl Delhousaye reviewed the book from a theological standpoint and provided valuable suggestions.

Bill Sellner, who God put in my life years ago to show me what God's grace and walking in the Spirit looks like. And his wife Elaine and her women's group, who gave valuable feedback as they went through *The Abiding Room* study.

Larry Winhold, whose reading and suggestions on an early version of the manuscript led to a chapter being discarded and a better one being written.

Bert Harned and Barry Seifert, my mentors, whose wisdom and guidance in my life have played a role beyond what can be calculated.

Nina Taylor, Judy Duncan, Sue Southern, and Jerry and Jean Anne Powers, true prayer warriors, whose prayers have encouraged and protected me and my family for over two decades.

Welcome to *The Abiding Room*

My wife looked at me pleasantly perplexed. "What's happened to your anger? You're not tense with me anymore. Something's happening to you. You're not the same."

Her words took me by surprise. I'd been unaware that any change had taken place in me since I'd spun into yet another rage a few months earlier. This time my anger had reached a new level. I'd really lost it, smashing a dish to pieces on the tile floor in front of Juli and our four-year-old son, Daniel. My action shocked her and sent him into hysterics.

This dish-smashing incident had opened my eyes to the damage my anger was causing, and I'd been fearful of what my future held. But I had no idea how to change the way I'd been living for forty years.

What I didn't know was that God had already begun doing a major work in my heart. After ten years as a Christian, I was starting to experience a life-changing, spiritual transformation—and Juli had noticed even though I hadn't. God had initiated a miracle, and our lives would never be the same. By God's grace and Juli's prayers, I discovered the abiding, Spirit-filled life.

As I learned to live by the power of the Holy Spirit over the next few years, I transformed from a husband whose bullying caused my wife to cry herself to sleep on many occasions to one whose marriage became a joyful experience for us both. Our family environment today is one our adult children enjoy coming home to.

Unfortunately, too few Christians are experiencing this abiding, Spirit-filled life. When God first opened my eyes to this new way of living, I asked a few long-term Jesus-followers I respect a question: "What percentage of the Christians you know do you believe are living in the power of the Holy Spirit?" They all estimated only about 5 percent. While there's no way to know the exact figure, their viewpoint that a very small minority of Christians experience the abiding life God has planned for us has been repeatedly confirmed to me over the past two decades. That's both unfortunate and unnecessary.

Since 2000, I've discipled young men and taught classes about the Abiding Room to people of all ages at my local church. I've found that regardless of where people are in their spiritual journey, the illustrations and diagrams I've developed can help them understand and experience the fullness of the Holy Spirit in new ways. And in this book, the biblical lessons I'm continuing to learn so I can live them out on a daily basis are explained, laying out the secrets to truths that can lead you to spiritual breakthrough as well.

We'll examine the three separate and distinct ways to live—or as we'll call it, The 3 Levels of Life. These three levels are described throughout the Bible in both the Old and New Testaments. Our hope is to live in the third level, in the Abiding Room, experiencing the abiding, Spirit-filled life.

At the end of each chapter you'll find these sections:

- *Abiding Truth*—These statements summarize the core message from each chapter.
- *Reflection Questions*—These questions and prompts are designed to help you think deeply about what you've just read and how to apply it to your life. Don't skip over this section. Ask the Holy Spirit to reveal to you how you can experience him in a new way. Take time to let him show you how the principles of each chapter are relevant to you and your life situations, and make notes in the space provided.
- *Song Suggestions*—These selected contemporary songs can help you further reflect on the application of each chapter's lessons in your own life. The following QR codes include links to all of the songs in one single playlist.

Welcome to *The Abiding Room*

Playlist Using Apple Music

Playlist Using Spotify

It's important for you to go through this book chapter by chapter. Understanding the connection *between* each chapter is almost as important as understanding the content *within* each chapter. You'll likely find many of the questions that arise are answered in subsequent chapters.

In appendix 5 you'll find a Suggested 12-Week Group Schedule. This outline provides a practical way for you to go through the entire book with a small group or class with a 12-week timeframe.

God's intention is for every follower of Jesus to experience the fruit of the Holy Spirit described in Galatians 5—love, joy, peace, patience, kindness, goodness, faithfulness, gentleness, and self-control. These are the wonderful blessings of Spirit-filled living we're about to explore. You can also come to know God's will for your life even better as you experience the presence of Jesus and the power of the Holy Spirit.

I'm confident the information and diagrams you're about to encounter will bless you with a fresh understanding of these wonderful truths.

And I pray they will allow you to experience the joy and peace of living by the power of the Holy Spirit on a daily basis—in your family, in your work, and in your church.

> May the God of hope fill you with
> all joy and peace in believing, so that by the
> power of the Holy Spirit you may abound in hope.
> (Romans 15:13)

Before you go any further, please visit the Abiding Room website at abidingroom.com and watch my chocolate milk video where I illustrate The 3 Levels of Life on the home page. This short video has been very popular with students. It will help you to quickly understand The 3 Levels of Life and provide the foundation for the upcoming instruction on them.

Part One

THE 3 LEVELS OF LIFE

CHAPTER 1

The 3 Levels of Life in the Old Testament

Throughout the Bible, God has given us stories and instruction to show us that, at any particular moment, our relationship with him is at one of three levels. But it is only when we are in Level III, the Abiding Room, that we experience God in the fullness he intends for us.

Throughout this book, you will see your relationship with God illustrated in the Abiding Room diagram below and several variations of it. This will be explained in greater detail as we proceed through the book.

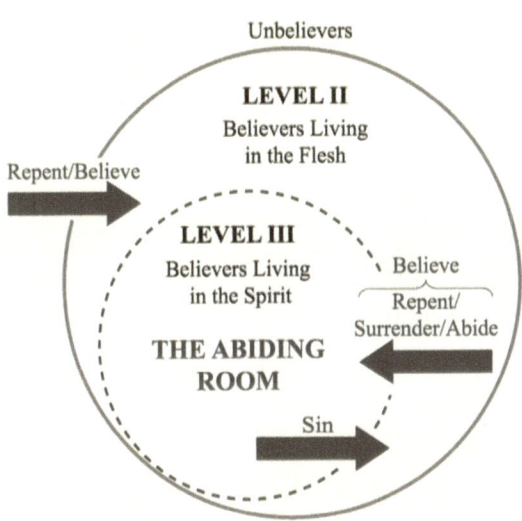

In this chapter, we will look at two Old Testament illustrations of The 3 Levels of Life: the garden of Eden and the journey of the Israelites.

THE GARDEN OF EDEN

The 3 Levels of Life first became a reality in the garden of Eden. In the beginning, mankind—the first being Adam and Eve—was sinless and walked in a harmonious relationship with God in the garden. God provided everything Adam and Eve needed. There was no death or separation between God and mankind because there was no sin.

So, there was only one level of life, as depicted in this diagram:

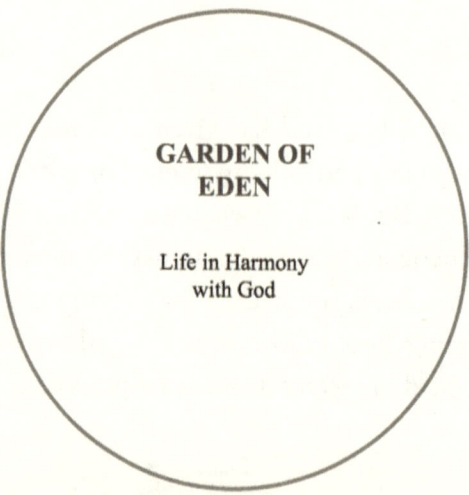

Life with God was how he intended it to be, but he gave Adam a command and a warning:

> And the Lord God commanded the man, saying, "You may surely eat of every tree of the garden, but of the tree of the knowledge of good and evil you shall not eat, for in the day that you eat of it **you shall surely die.**" (Genesis 2:16–17)

Then Satan deceived Adam and Eve, and they disobeyed God by eating from the one tree forbidden to them. The perfect, harmonious relationship between God, who was and is perfect and holy, and mankind, who was now sinful, was broken. And because God is holy, he gave mankind consequences for sin.

One of those consequences was Adam and Eve could no longer live in the garden of Eden:

> So, the LORD God banished him from the Garden of Eden to work the ground from which he had been taken. After he drove the man out, he placed on the east side of the Garden of Eden Cherubim and a flaming sword slashing back and forth to guard the way to the tree of life. (Genesis 3:23–24 NIV)

So, then there were two levels of life, as shown in the next diagram:

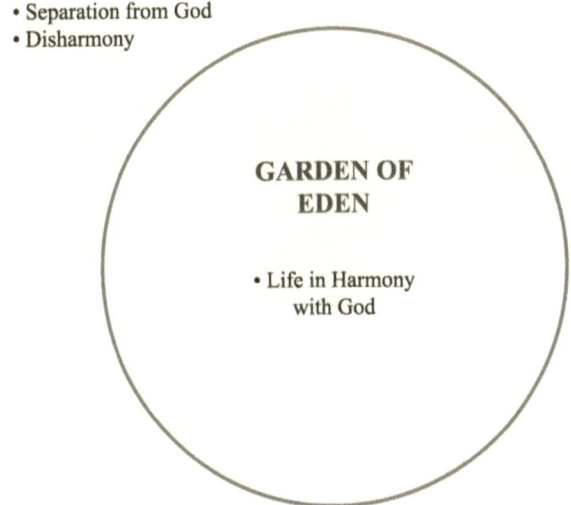

Ultimately, Adam and Eve's sin led to another consequence: an end to life itself for every person.

> And the LORD God said, "The man has now become like one of us, knowing good and evil. He must not be allowed to reach out his hand and take also from the tree of life and eat, and live forever." (Genesis 3:22 NIV)

> Altogether, Adam lived a total of 930 years, and then he died. (Genesis 5:5 NIV)

So, there became The 3 Levels of Life, as the diagram below illustrates.

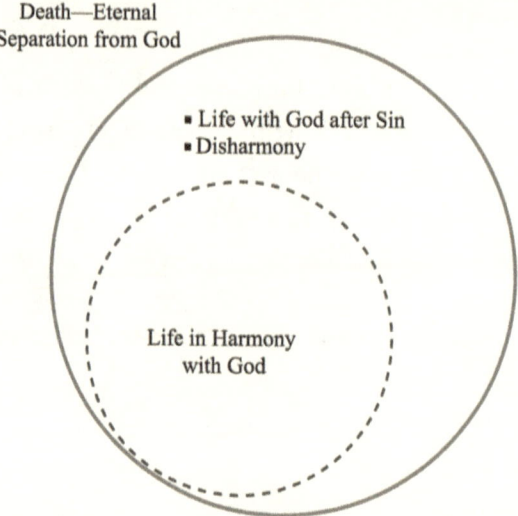

The Bible tells us sin still impacts *all* humankind today:

Therefore, just as sin came into the world through one man, and death through sin, and so death spread to **all men** because all sinned. (Romans 5:12)

The entire Bible shows us our relationship with God is at one of three levels. As we shall see, only one of the three levels of life is truly pleasing to God—when we live in harmony with him. Unfortunately, few people are consistently living this way.

THE JOURNEY OF THE ISRAELITES

Perhaps you're familiar with the story of Moses leading the Israelites out of Egypt that is found in the book of Exodus, chapters 1–14.

Egypt had held the Israelites captive and worked them as slaves for over 400 years. But God heard the cries of his people and instructed Moses to confront Pharaoh. After ten plagues, Pharaoh let God's people go.

Once the Israelites departed, however, Pharaoh changed his mind and pursued them with his army. In one of the greatest miracles in history, God parted the Red Sea, allowing his people to walk through it on dry ground with walls of water on either side. Pharaoh's army chased after them onto the dry floor of the Red Sea, but after the Israelites had safely crossed to the other side, God caused the waters to flow back, drowning all those in pursuit.

Having saved the Israelites from slavery under Pharaoh, God's intention was to take them into the Holy Land as he had promised. But they chose to not trust him, and because of their sin of unbelief, they spent forty years wandering in the desert. Then God appointed Joshua to finally lead them into the Holy Land, and once again he had them cross a body of water—the Jordan River.

The Israelites' journey took them through three distinct pieces of land: Egypt, the desert, and the Holy Land. As we'll now see, these three pieces of land represent The 3 Levels of Life in our relationship with God.

Leaving Egypt

Let's begin with God bringing the Israelites out of Egypt, across the Red Sea, and into the desert.

God paints a picture for us, with Moses representing a type of Christ, and Pharaoh representing a type of Satan. Egypt depicts a separation from God. The crossing of the Red Sea indicates God's love for us by sending Christ to save us from our sins.

Think for a moment about the name: the Red Sea. When you think of a body of water, what colors do you think of? I usually think of blue or gray or maybe green, but certainly not red!

I believe God created the Red Sea as a unique body of water to remind us of Jesus' blood on the cross. Jesus came into the world to save us, and he saved us by his blood. He saved us by his sacrificial death on the cross and resurrection. The Israelites going down into the Red Sea depicts death. But their coming through the Red Sea depicts rising up into life—separated and safe from Satan (Pharaoh).

The Red Sea is also quite large. It is about 1,400 miles long with a width of about 100 miles. The depth can range between 426 feet, to over 9,000 feet. In other words, it is such a vast and deep body of water that no one can cross it on foot unless God makes it possible.

I think God created the Red Sea enormous to illustrate his enormous love for us. The Red Sea, like God's love, is so wide and deep that people can never cross back over it on foot.

Once a person puts their faith in Jesus and becomes a child of God, they can never do anything to cross back over the Red Sea into Egypt with the unsaved; that is, back unto death. To allow anyone to cross back over or to force them back over the Red Sea would violate God's very nature because God is love.

> Anyone who does not love does not know God, because God is love. (1 John 4:8)

You can never lose your salvation, even when you sin. When you become a Christian, heaven is your home regardless of your subsequent behavior. There's nothing you can do to separate yourself from God's love. It is absolute and permanent regardless of your actions or behavior.

As you can see in the next diagram, the outer circle has just one arrow crossing over the Red Sea from Egypt into the desert. It's a one-way arrow because Christians have eternal security and can never go back. This illustrates God's *unconditional* love. And God's love is unconditional because God *is* love.

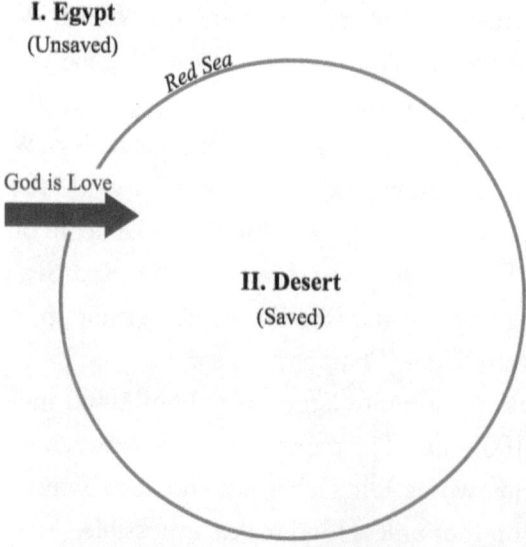

The Desert and the Holy Land

When the Israelites crossed through the Red Sea and into the desert, God did not intend for them to remain there. He intended for them to enter the Holy Land he had promised them.

> "And he brought us **out** from there, that he might bring us **in** and give us the land that he swore to give to our fathers." (Deuteronomy 6:23)

The next diagram illustrates this entire movement.

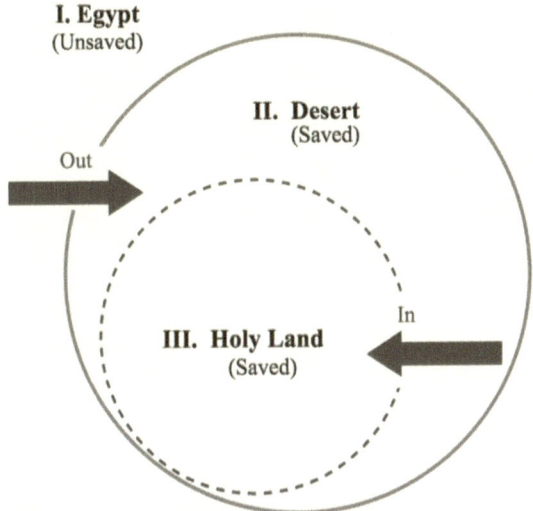

The desert illustrates Level II: saved but living in the flesh. Again, God didn't intend for the Israelites to wander in the desert but intended for them to enter the Holy Land. Likewise, God doesn't intend for us to live in the flesh. He intends for us to enter the next, and best, level of life—living by the power of the Holy Spirit.

The movement from Level II to Level III is shown in the next diagram.

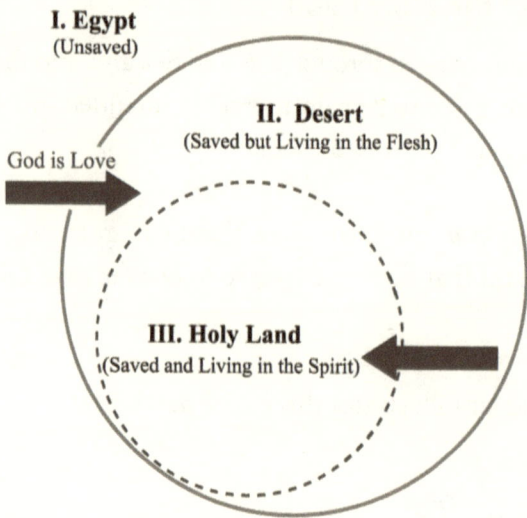

In the desert, God fed his children with water and manna, but he described the Holy Land as a land flowing with milk and honey. As the Israelites found out, it was no picnic living in the desert while drinking and eating nothing but water and manna. While God continually provided for their needs regardless of the extent of their daily faithfulness or unfaithfulness (just as he does for ours today), his people longed for something more.

How many followers of Jesus today are longing for something more as well? That longing is our desire to live filled, led, and empowered by the Holy Spirit! God has blessed us with this desire so we will never stop seeking him.

What allows us to enter into and remain in the Holy Land? That is, how can we enter into God's presence and experience the power of the Holy Spirit? Again, God shows us what is required of us through the journey of the Israelites.

> "If the LORD is **pleased with us,** he will lead us into that land, a land flowing with milk and honey, and will give it to us." (Numbers 14:8 NIV)

God is pleased with us when we are living by the power of the Holy Spirit, rather than in our flesh. In the New Testament, the apostle Paul tells us that, "Those who are in the **flesh cannot please God**." (Romans 8:8)

Why can't the flesh please God? The apostle Paul answers that question: "For I know that **nothing good** dwells in me, that is, **in my flesh**. For I have the desire to do what is right, but not the ability to carry it out" (Romans 7:18).

As we see in Numbers 14:8, what was necessary for the Israelites to enter the Holy Land was to be pleasing to God. But as we also see in Romans 8:8, since there's nothing good in our flesh, when we are operating in the flesh, we are not completely pleasing to our Holy God.

We see this illustrated in the following diagram:

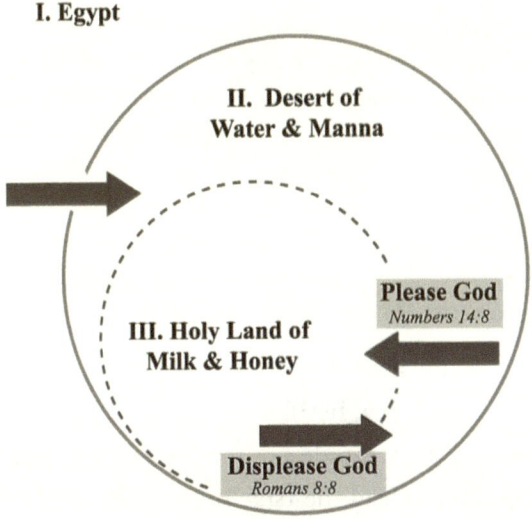

So, while God's love is unconditional, his pleasure is conditional. Why is God's pleasure conditional? Because God is holy. We'll explore the importance of God's holiness in greater detail in chapter 13, but for now we'll focus on the fact that, though God's love is constant and permanent, his pleasure with us is conditionally based on the choices we make.

That is what the Israelites discovered when God explained to them:

"For I am the LORD your God. Consecrate yourselves therefore, and **be holy for I am holy** … for I am the LORD who brought you up out of the land of Egypt to be your God. You shall therefore **be holy, for I am holy.**" (Leviticus 11:44–45)

God's love and holiness are illustrated in the next diagram.

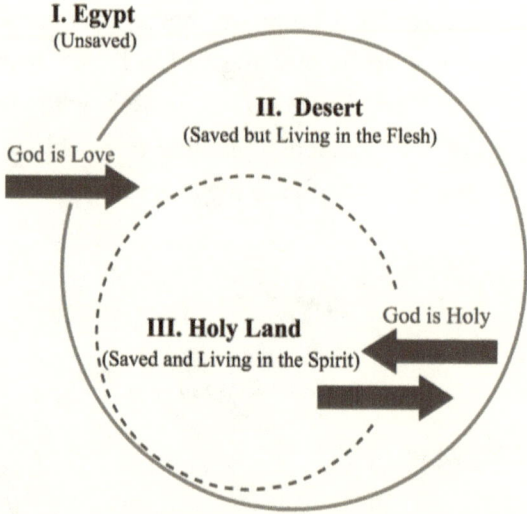

Crossing the Jordan River

Similar to how God illustrated his *love* in saving us through the Israelites' crossing of the Red Sea, he illustrated his *holiness* using the Jordan River. After wandering in the desert for forty years, and Moses' death, God instructed Joshua to lead the Israelites into the Holy Land by crossing the Jordan River.

> After the death of Moses the servant of the LORD, the LORD said to Joshua the son of Nun, Moses assistant, "Moses my servant is dead. Now therefore arise, go over this Jordan, you and all this people, into the land that I am giving to them, to the people of Israel." (Joshua 1:1–2)

The 3 Levels of Life in the Old Testament

The Jordan River is about 200 miles long with a width of about 90 to 100 feet. Depending on where you stand, the depth can range from three to ten feet. In other words, the Jordan River is nothing like the Red Sea. It's shallow and narrow enough so that, unlike the Red Sea, a person can wade across it.

The Israelites' crossing the Jordan River into the Holy Land is symbolic of our entering God's most intimate presence—when we are abiding in Christ and walking in the Spirit.

Unlike the Red Sea however, the Jordan River *can* be crossed back over into the desert by anyone if they so choose. God gave us a shallow, narrow, physical Jordan River that we can choose to cross back over into the desert, to illustrate that in our spiritual life we may choose to go our own way through sin.

But this means moving out of God's intimate presence and living in the flesh. For God to allow us to continue in sin and still remain in his intimate presence would violate God's very nature, because God is holy.

Still, God's grace remains. He continues to be merciful and shower his grace upon us even in our shortcomings.

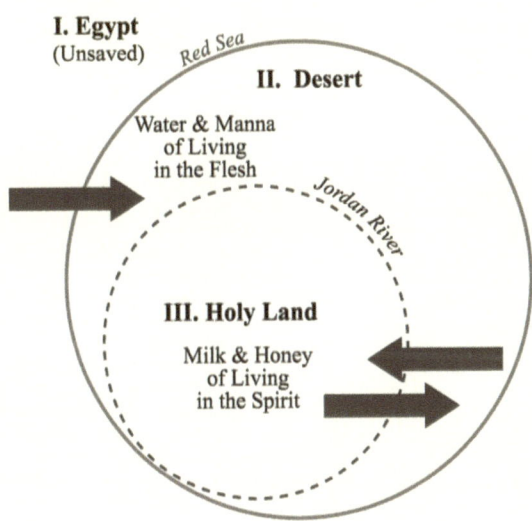

And so, through the journey of the Israelites, we again see the illustration of The 3 Levels of Life. We see we have the assurance of our salvation (one-way arrow) because God is love. But we also see the depth of our relationship with God is conditional upon our life choices (two-way arrow) because God is holy.

ABIDING TRUTH

The Old Testament establishes and illustrates
The 3 Levels of Life.

NOTE: If you do not have the peace of knowing you will spend eternity with God in heaven, I invite you to read appendix 1 now to learn how you can have that assurance.

REFLECTION QUESTIONS

1. What do you think the story of Adam and Eve tells us about ourselves as people, about the enemy and his schemes, and about God?

2. How do we fall prey to the same type of temptations as Adam and Eve when we seek to live in harmony with God?

3. Where is the folly in thinking, *If I had God right in front of me as the Israelites did, this whole thing would be a lot easier?*

4. What circumstances did you find yourself in the last time you were in a desert with God? How did you change what you were doing to reconnect (abide) with him?

5. Explain your understanding of The 3 Levels of Life and where you currently find yourself. (There is no wrong answer here!)

6. How do you think you can find yourself abiding in Jesus more often? There is no one right answer here, so be creative.

The 3 Levels of Life in the Old Testament

SONG SUGGESTIONS

"Egypt" by Bethel Music, featuring Cory Asbury
"No Longer Slaves" by Bethel Music, featuring Jonathan David and Melissa Helser
"Perfectly Loved" by Rachel Lampa, featuring Toby Mac

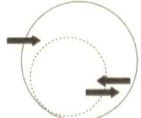

CHAPTER 2

The 3 Levels of Life in the New Testament

In chapter 1, we saw how the Old Testament illustrated The 3 Levels of Life. The New Testament also illustrates The 3 Levels of Life. Let's look at two examples found in Romans and 1 Corinthians.

ROMANS 7 AND 8

How did you become a Christian? You repented and believed.

> Jesus came into Galilee, proclaiming the gospel of God and saying, "The time is fulfilled, and the kingdom of God is at hand; **repent and believe** in the gospel." (Mark 1:14–15)

You were an unbeliever, accepted Jesus' invitation, and became a believer. As we discussed in chapter 1, your salvation is a one-way trip! You never have to fear losing your salvation. It is a done deal. Jesus says you have eternal security because he and God the Father have you securely in their grip.

> "I give them eternal life, and they shall never perish; **no one will snatch them out of my hand**. My Father, who has given them to me, is greater than all; **no one can snatch them out of my Father's hand**." (John 10:28–29 NIV)

The Bible also tells us you can know with absolute certainty you have eternal security through the Holy Spirit. Upon conversion, you received the Holy Spirit to indwell you forever. He will never be taken away from you.

When you believed, you were marked in him with **a seal, the promised Holy Spirit,** who is a deposit **guaranteeing our inheritance** until the redemption of those who are God's possession—to the praise of his glory. (Ephesians 1:13–14 NIV)

The one-way arrow in the following diagram illustrates the assurance of your salvation.

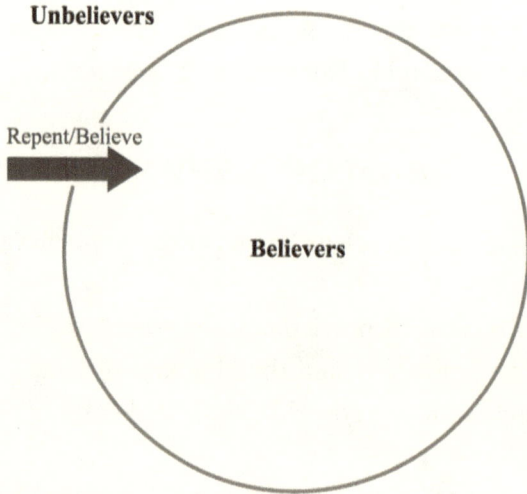

Living in the Flesh

With full confidence in our salvation, we then choose moment-by-moment to live in either the flesh or the Spirit. The apostle Paul tells us in the book of Romans about his own spiritual journey. He confides that it can be a difficult process, even for him. In Romans 7, Paul describes his struggles when he is living in the flesh.

For I do not understand my own actions. For I do not do what I want, but I do the very thing I hate. (Romans 7:15)

For I know that nothing good dwells in me, that is, in my flesh. For I have the desire to do what is right, but not the ability to carry it out. For I do not do the good I want, but the evil I do not want is what I keep on doing. (Romans 7:18–19)

Paul even cries out in desperation, in Romans 7:24, "Wretched man that I am! Who will deliver me from this body of death?" Have you ever felt like that? I know I have!

Living in the Spirit

However, in Romans 8, Paul enthusiastically describes the life of freedom and victory you, too, can experience as you live by the power of the Holy Spirit. When you are living in the Spirit, you can live free of sin and experience peace.

There is therefore now no condemnation for those who are in Christ Jesus. For the law of **the Spirit of life has set you free** in Christ Jesus from the law of sin and death. (Romans 8:1–2)

For those who live according to the flesh set their minds on the things of flesh, but those who live according to the Spirit set their minds on the things of the Spirit. For to set the mind on the flesh is death, but to set the mind on **the Spirit is life and peace.** (Romans 8:5–6)

Through the apostle Paul's personal testimony, we can see The 3 Levels of Life. The following diagram illustrates Romans 7 and 8:

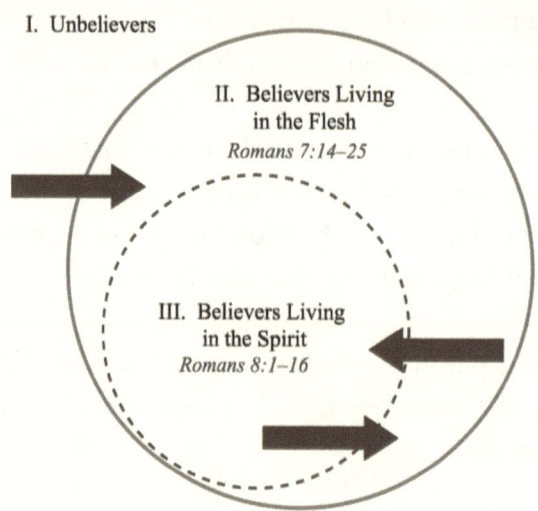

1 CORINTHIANS 2 AND 3

Have you ever wondered if you can really know what God desires you to do? You can! When you are living in the Abiding Room, it is possible for you to know what he is instructing you to do.

God illustrates The 3 Levels of Life through the words of Paul in the book of 1 Corinthians as he describes the three types of people in the world. Let's look at Paul's words to the Corinthian church.

Level I—The Natural Person

> The **natural person** does not accept the things of the Spirit of God, for they are folly to him, and he is **not able to understand** them because they are spiritually discerned. (1 Corinthians 2:14)

Level II—The Fleshly Person

> But I, brothers, could not address you as spiritual people, but as **people of the flesh,** as infants in Christ. I fed you with milk, not solid food, for you were **not ready** for it. And even now you are not yet ready, for you are still of the flesh. For while there is jealousy and strife among you, are you not of the flesh and behaving only in a human way? (1 Corinthians 3:1–4)

Level III—The Spiritual Person

> The **spiritual person** judges all things, but is himself to be judged by no one. "For who has understood the mind of the Lord so as to instruct him?" But we **have the mind of Christ**. (1 Corinthians 2:15–16)

In 1 Corinthians 2 and 3, Paul writes to the church at Corinth, recounting his previous visit and teachings there. He very clearly describes three types of people in terms of their spiritual state. His explanations are relevant and important to us today.

In 1 Corinthians 2, Paul first distinguishes between the two extremes: The unbeliever (Level I), whom he calls the natural person, and the believer living in the Spirit, whom he calls the spiritual person (Level III).

The unbelieving, Level I natural person cannot understand the things of God because they do not have the Holy Spirit. The things of God are foolishness to them. The spiritual, Level III person however, *can* understand the things of God because the Holy Spirit reveals them to them.

Then in chapter 3, Paul places the Corinthian church squarely in the middle, at Level II. They're undoubtedly saved, but they're also definitely not spiritually minded, oriented, or discerning.

While Paul has acknowledged the Corinthians are believing brothers and sisters, he describes them as fleshly—mere infants. Since they're more like worldly unbelievers in their hearts than Spirit-led believers, they're unable to understand the richness and fullness of God's message in their minds. As a result, Paul has to talk to them in Level II "baby" terms. Both individually and collectively, these worldly Level II believers are living at a lower spiritual level than they should be. Therefore, they're unable to comprehend many of the things of God.

Not only are these Level II fleshly believers unable to comprehend spiritual truths, in addition, they're also *acting* like unbelievers. Their chocolate syrup has settled to the bottom of the glass rather than being stirred up. Their actions are causing problems within the church itself, namely jealousy and quarreling. Their fleshly living is causing church conflict. Sound familiar?

Though he would rather be delving into the richness of the truths and wisdom of God with them, Paul instead has to go into church problem-solving mode in his teaching and address their misbehavior. He uses phrases like "not ready" and "still of the flesh," implying this is not a permanent spiritual condition, but rather a matter of choice. Paul desires his listeners to cross over from Level II to Level III, as shown in the next diagram.

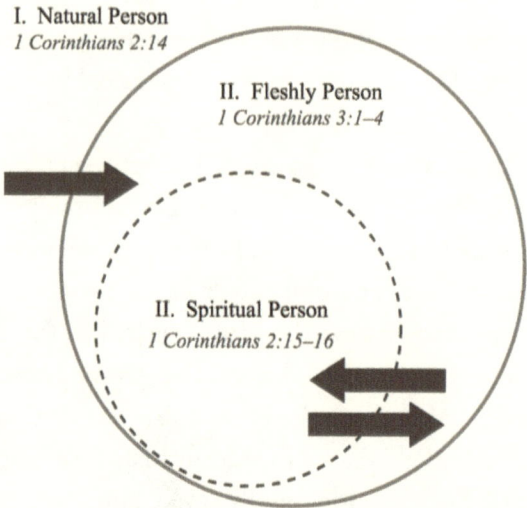

It's not that the Corinthians are not equipped; it's that they're choosing not to utilize the "equipment" they have—the person of the Holy Spirit. It's not that they're not talented or gifted enough, it's that they're not appropriating what they've been gifted—the person of the Holy Spirit. It's not that they don't have what it takes, it's that they aren't taking advantage of who they already have—the person of the Holy Spirit!

Everything Paul said to the Corinthians applies to each of us today. Just as the Corinthians had a choice to live in the Spirit or in the flesh, so do you. You don't have to live in Level II. When you enter into Level III, the Abiding Room, you, too, are spiritual, rather than fleshly. You are able to live in harmony with God and others. You are with Jesus, led by the Holy Spirit, and have the mind of Christ. Jesus gives you a clearer understanding of why you exist as he reveals to you his plan and purpose for your life!

So, through 1 Corinthians 2 and 3, we see once again The 3 Levels of Life.

A Word about the Limitations of Diagrams

In chapters 1 and 2, we've seen four separate biblical examples of The 3 Levels of Life and diagrams illustrating them. At this point, it's important to remember these diagrams are merely simple illustrations of the three distinct levels of life derived from the Bible. They depict the difference between living by the power of the Holy Spirit versus living in the weakness of the flesh.

The diagram has two circles. The outer circle is a solid line representing a spiritual boundary requiring an act of God to cross, while the innermost circle is a line of dashes representing a spiritual boundary only requiring the will of men and women to repeatedly cross over and back again.

But while the diagrams and terms used in the illustrations are based on the Bible, they are presentations that can only be shown as absolutes. That is, they depict our spiritual condition as all or nothing—as completely one way or the other. We are either completely in Level I, II, or III.

Let's examine this a bit further, so it doesn't impede our upcoming discussions.

With respect to Level I versus Level II—saved or not saved—the diagrams accurately depict a spiritual reality—everyone is either saved or not saved. We are either fully inside or fully outside of the larger circle. We are either children of God destined for heaven, or we are not.

Comparing whether we as followers of Jesus are in Level II or Level III at any moment, however, is a bit trickier. While the diagrams are instructive, they imply we are either living completely in the flesh, in Level II, or we are living completely in the Spirit, in Level III. In reality, most of life, including our spiritual walk, is not nearly as clear. We live in uncertain shades of gray.

When you think about it, though, the Bible *is* absolute in many places, including comparing life in the Spirit versus life in the flesh. For instance, the all-or-nothing phrase, "filled with the Spirit," is used numerous times in the Bible. There's no instance where the Bible describes someone as "partially filled" or "mostly filled." Likewise, though the terms and illustrations used in *The Abiding Room* are biblically based, they will always fail to be completely adequate in describing our spiritual walk in this physical, fallen world. *The Abiding Room's* instructions and diagrams are merely tools intended to open our eyes and guide us to a fuller relationship with God.

So while the words and diagrams attempt to convey the essential elements of the abiding, Spirit-filled life as completely as possible, we must acknowledge their capability of explaining the wonderful mysteries of these spiritual truths is limited.

Now, let's move on and explore the wonderful truths of the Holy Spirit!

ABIDING TRUTH

The New Testament confirms and illustrates
The 3 Levels of Life.

REFLECTION QUESTIONS

1. There are many great ways to prepare ourselves so the world has less sway to pull us back into living in the flesh. Romans 13:14 tells us, "Clothe yourselves with the Lord Jesus Christ." What does this mean to you?

2. Identify one way you often find yourself moving from abiding to living in the flesh. What can you do to defeat it in the future?

3. Some would argue that if living in the flesh is not harmful to others, then it's not necessarily causing a problem in your relationship with God. Based on what you have learned in this chapter, how might God view this perspective and why should we be on our guard to avoid justifying "fleshly" behavior?

4. Think of when you were new in your faith as compared to now. What are some of the ways you view your development toward spiritual maturity now that are different than when you started?

5. What are some of the ways you have found to regularly impact your development toward spiritual maturity?

6. What are the consequences of not planning to grow within your faith? How does that have an impact outside of your own life?

The 3 Levels of Life in the New Testament

SONG SUGGESTIONS

"The Struggle" by Tenth Avenue North
"Let It Fade" by Jeremy Camp
"All You Got" by DC Talk

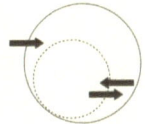

Part Two

THE HOLY SPIRIT

CHAPTER 3

The Battle of the Spirit and the Flesh

> But I say, walk by the Spirit, and you will not gratify the desires of the flesh. For the desires of the flesh are against the Spirit, and the desires of the Spirit are against the flesh, for these are opposed to each other, to keep you from doing the things you want to do. (Galatians 5:16–17)

Did you know you're in an ongoing, daily, spiritual battle? As Galatians 5:16–17 tells us, not only are the Spirit and the flesh opposites, but they're also opponents. And they are engaged in a battle for our hearts. Essentially, there is a spiritual civil war raging inside of us. It is a major battle for everything God wants you to become.

As followers of Jesus, moment-by-moment, we are all choosing to either have our chocolate syrup "stirred up" and be empowered by the Spirit or be impaired by the flesh. When our hearts are led by the Spirit, our lives exhibit the fruit of the Spirit, and we look like Jesus to others. But when we are living in our flesh, we look a lot like the world. Is it any wonder Satan will do everything he can to keep us from walking in the Spirit?

This internal battle between the indwelling Holy Spirit and your flesh is going on every minute of every day. And although the battle never ends in this life, you can consistently win the daily fight. It helps to know the enemy and understand what is at stake. In this chapter we'll examine this internal conflict to set the stage for the upcoming chapters that describe the many blessings available to you when you win this fight.

Evidence of the Spiritual Battle—the Flesh

> Now the works of the flesh are **evident**: sexual immorality, impurity, sensuality, idolatry, sorcery, **enmity, strife, jealousy, fits of anger, rivalries, dissensions, divisions, envy, drunkenness**, orgies, and things like these. I warn you, as I warned you before, that those who do such things will not inherit the kingdom of God. (Galatians 5:19–21)

When you read some of those terms used by the apostle Paul in the preceding verses describing the flesh in his letter to the Galatian church, perhaps you can say they don't describe your experience. But look again at the bolded words in the middle of the verses. Do some of those actions describe your life? Your family? Have you heard of churches experiencing strife (conflict or bitter disagreement) over fundamental issues? How about jealousy, fits of anger, rivalries, dissensions, divisions, or envy in the church?

The flesh is destructive to relationships of all kinds. Unfortunately, works of the flesh are far too common among followers of Jesus. They existed in Paul's day, 2,000 years ago, and they still exist today.

Notice how Paul describes the reality of living in the flesh—it is highly visible to others. He says, "the works of the flesh are **evident**" (verse 19). If it's true that a large majority of believers today spend the bulk of each day living in the flesh rather than living in the Spirit, it not only creates difficulties in our lives, but it is "evident" to the outside, watching world too.

Evidence of the Spiritual Battle—the Holy Spirit

> But the fruit of the Spirit is love, joy, peace, patience, kindness, goodness, faithfulness, gentleness, [and] self-control. (Galatians 5:22–23)

After explaining the works of the flesh, Paul contrasts them with the fruit of the Spirit. The evidence that you are living in the Spirit is that the fruit of the Spirit is exhibited in your life.

Before you received Jesus as your Savior, you always operated in your flesh—never in the Spirit. Because you didn't have the indwelling Holy

Spirit, you had no choice to live otherwise. But when you received Jesus as your Savior, you also received the Holy Spirit. And that means you no longer must live by your flesh. You can *choose* to live every moment by the power of the Holy Spirit.

Nothing Good in the Flesh

In contrasting the Spirit and the flesh, Jesus says, "It is the Spirit who gives life; the **flesh** counts for **nothing**; the words that I have spoken to you are spirit and are life" (John 6:63 NIV).

Again, the apostle Paul said, "For I know that **nothing** good dwells in me, that is, in my **flesh**. For I have the desire to do what is right, but not the ability to carry it out" (Romans 7:18).

In both verses we see a link between the two words "flesh" and "nothing." These verses do *not* say there are "some things wrong with the flesh" or there are "some things good in the flesh." They do *not* say the flesh is "imperfect" (that could imply there is something of merit or value that can be coaxed out of the flesh). Rather, the Bible clearly says there is *nothing* good in our flesh. *Nothing.*

Our flesh is not 90 percent good; it's not 50 percent good; it's not even 20 percent good. It is 0 percent good. Our flesh is completely flawed and depraved. It is what Jesus paid the price for on the cross by his death. Our flesh cannot be improved into something good because there is nothing good in our flesh in the first place.

When we're living in the flesh, we want to get our way. But when we're walking in union with the Holy Spirit, we are servant-hearted. Maybe it's no coincidence that "flesh" spelled backward with the *h* removed is "self." Our flesh wants what it wants when it wants it. It operates to please self, or what has been called the unholy trinity—Me, Myself, and I.

How Do You Know if You Are Walking in the Spirit?

How do you know if you're being led by the Spirit at any given moment? Well, let me ask you this: How do you know an orange tree is an orange tree? By its fruit, of course. And that's how you know if you are living in the Spirit or the flesh.

If a personal spiritual examination reveals the fruit of the Spirit—love, joy, peace, patience, kindness, gentleness, and self-control—you can be confident you are living in the Spirit. But if the examination reveals the deeds of the flesh, you're living in the flesh.

Jesus described it this way: "Make a tree good and its fruit will be good, or make a tree bad and its fruit will be bad, for a tree is recognized by its fruit" (Matthew 12:33 NIV). And he said it's impossible for us to bear good fruit when we're operating in the bad tree of the flesh: "Likewise, every good tree bears good fruit, but a bad tree bears bad fruit. A good tree cannot bear bad fruit, and a bad tree cannot bear good fruit" (Matthew 7:17–18 NIV).

If we're producing bad fruit, we need to get to the *root* of the problem—we're operating in the flesh. Trying and striving to produce good spiritual fruit from a bad, fleshly root simply will not work. Why? Because there's nothing good *in* the flesh, so nothing good can come *out* of the flesh. Self-effort cannot rectify the situation because self cannot overcome the flesh.

The bad fruit produced by the flesh is not merely bad behavior that needs correction; it's the external evidence of an internal heart problem. It's not the behavior that needs to be addressed; it's the heart itself. That's the cause of the problem. The heart operating in the flesh rather than by the power of the Holy Spirit does not need a topical salve. It needs internal heart surgery.

By God's grace, however, when we are letting Jesus live out his life in and through us by the power of the Holy Spirit, we can resemble good trees bearing good fruit.

Consequences of Living in the Flesh

Living in the flesh leads to sin, and sin has consequences. This impacts our lives in the following three areas:

1. *Our relationship with God.* Our holy God cannot look upon sin and be pleased.

> For the mind that is set on the flesh is hostile to God, for it does not submit to God's law; indeed, it cannot. Those who are in the flesh **cannot please** God. (Romans 8:7–8)

The Battle of the Spirit and the Flesh

We experience the impact of sin in our relationship with God through what the Bible calls "grieving" the Holy Spirit.

> And do not **grieve** the Holy Spirit of God, by whom you were sealed for the day of redemption. (Ephesians 4:30)

The Holy Spirit is a person, and since he is God, he is holy. Sin grieves the person of the Holy Spirit and hinders us from experiencing the fullness of our relationship with God. When we sin and feel an ache in our hearts, that is the Holy Spirit convicting us of sin.

When the Holy Spirit is grieved by our sin, he then notifies us so we can correct our course. He lovingly directs us to confess, repent, and quickly turn back to and connect with Jesus. Our quick obedience to his prompting lessens the chance of a lengthy, internal agony as a result of the sin and its consequences.

When we choose to live in our flesh and not in the Spirit, we wander in the spiritual desert. We live fleshly, Level II lives, rather than Spirit-filled, Level III lives.

It is important, however, to remember and have confidence in our eternal security as depicted by the one-way Repent/Believe arrow that shows us moving out of Level I living into Level II. That way, when we sin and experience the grieving of the Holy Spirit in our hearts, we know it is the Spirit convicting us. He is giving us a godly sorrow meant to lead us to repentance and restore the fullness of our relationship with Jesus.

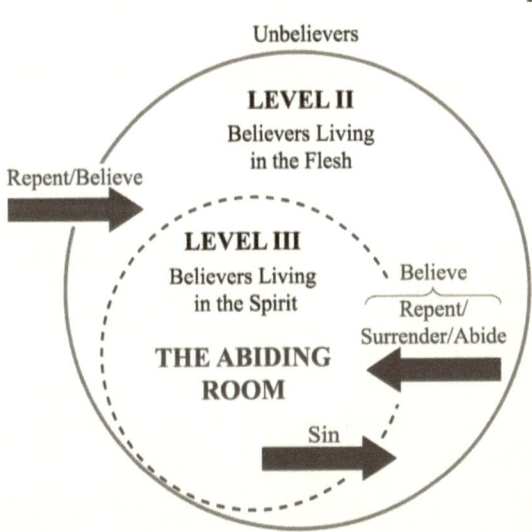

2. *Our relationships with others.* The flesh produces enmity, strife, jealousy, fits of anger, rivalries, dissensions, divisions, and envy between people. As we saw in chapter 2, the apostle Paul was unable to preach about the deeper things of God to the Corinthian church because of their fleshly living. He had to first address the problems between the members in their church.

If it is true, and I believe it is, that today a minority of Christians are walking in the Spirit at any given time, then most followers of Jesus are operating in the flesh most of the time. As a result, too much time is spent on conflict resolution within churches instead of focusing on impacting people outside of the church. The consequences are extremely detrimental within churches, and they lessen the positive impact they should be having upon a needy, hurting, and lost world. Christians living fleshly lives was a significant problem in the church in Paul's day and continues to be a problem today.

3. *The peace within us.* When we walk in harmony with the Holy Spirit, we experience joy and peace. But when we walk in the flesh, that joy and peace are lost as we grieve the Spirit. Fortunately, God has absolutely no intention of leaving us there. He is always at work to draw us and welcome us back into intimate fellowship with him.

God's Grace Abounds

When we operate in the flesh, it does not mean God can't use us for his purposes. Thankfully, God is gracious and patient with us, and he can work through us even when we are not being led by the Holy Spirit at any moment.

Let me share an example of how God used me on a particular occasion, even though I was definitely living in my flesh. One afternoon, I was relaxing in my parked car in a public parking lot casually going through emails on my phone with no immediate time pressures. The car door was open and a stranger walked up and began talking to me. Though I had nowhere to be, after ten minutes I was looking for a way to get rid of him.

Then an idea that seemed like an effective way to get him to leave occurred to me. I simply asked him, "Who do you say Jesus is?"

To my great surprise he answered, "Well, they say he's the Son of God."

Immediately, the Holy Spirit impressed upon me that God was at work. So I set my phone aside, and within a few minutes this gentleman had prayed to receive Christ and committed to obtaining a Bible and going to church! He explained to me how his daughter and son-in-law had been sharing the gospel with him for years, but he had resisted their invitations to receive Christ into his life.

Although I was operating completely in the flesh when this man approached me, God orchestrated a divine meeting between the two of us. Ironically, he chose to use my fleshly motive to ask this man a pointed question—a question he then used to bring this man to a saving faith in Jesus!

God is able to work through us even when we are living in the flesh. It's not that we're *useless* to God when we're in the flesh, it's that we're *less useful* to him.

The Harmonious Spirit-Led Church

> And all who believed were together and had all things in common. And they were selling their possessions and belongings and distributing the proceeds to all, as any had need. And day by day, attending the temple together and breaking bread in their homes, they received their food with glad and generous hearts, praising God and having favor with all the people. And the Lord added to their number day by day those who were being saved. (Acts 2:44–47)

This description of the church just after Pentecost paints a desirable picture of what a church led by the Holy Spirit looks like. The people were harmoniously meeting together in both the temple and each other's homes and showing great generosity toward each other. Many unbelievers were taking notice of the church as they saw the unity of its people and as the Holy Spirit opened their eyes to the good news of salvation through Jesus.

An Encouraging Reminder

As a follower of Jesus, you are God's masterpiece. You are his best creation because he made you in his very image. You are his child whom he loves unconditionally. And as your heavenly Father, he wants the best for you. That means he wants to teach you to consistently walk in his Spirit.

Regardless of whether you are led by the Spirit or the flesh at any particular moment, it has absolutely no impact on God's infinite and eternal love for you. Even when you live in the flesh, he loves you just the same as when you're living in the Spirit. No amount of fleshly living will ever separate you from God's infinite love for you, his beloved child. But when you learn to consistently live by the power of the Holy Spirit, God can do things through you you've never imagined!

> I have loved you with an everlasting love; therefore I have continued my faithfulness to you. (Jeremiah 31:3)

Test Your Heart

Take some time to ask God for help in knowing your heart. Pray this timeless and heartfelt prayer from King David's heart:

> "Search me, O God, and know my heart;
> test me and know my anxious thoughts.
> See if there is any offensive way in me,
> and lead me in the way everlasting."
> (Psalm 139:23–24 NIV)

Every word of this passage has a piercing insight. God knows your heart no matter where you are physically, emotionally, or spiritually, and he rejoices when you come to him with this request. He longs to answer this prayer in order to draw you nearer to him.

ABIDING TRUTH

An internal battle between the indwelling Holy Spirit
and your flesh goes on every minute of every day,
but you can consistently win the daily fight
as you choose to walk in the Spirit.

REFLECTION QUESTIONS

1. Why do you think we, as well-meaning, devoted Christ-followers, slip into thoughts or habits that center around self? Why is this so easy?

2. How can you protect yourself from being snared by the desire to live in the flesh? How can you build a new habit of choosing to consistently walk in the Spirit instead of the flesh?

3. Imagine what your church body might be like if everyone walked in the Spirit on a more regular basis. How would this change the way people behave at church? At work? In their community?

4. Ask yourself how you could change one thing in your life you feel causes you to live in the flesh. This could be a habit, a relationship, or even a specific situation that stands outside of God's will for you. Once identified, make a plan for combating it, and then share this plan with someone you trust, asking them to pray for you.

SONG SUGGESTIONS

"Battle Belongs" by Phil Wickham
"Disappear" by Out of the Grey
"Death Was Arrested" by North Point Worship

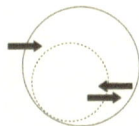

CHAPTER 4

Experiencing the Holy Spirit's Joy and Peace

The blessings of living in the Holy Spirit are quite stunning when you think about it. God has placed his Holy Spirit in you so you can live with joy and peace regardless of your circumstances. And the Holy Spirit gives you guidance and the power to carry out the work God has planned for you. This is truly the abundant life Jesus spoke of:

"I came that they may have life and have it abundantly." (John 10:10)

Even when the world around you is in chaos, by the presence and power of the Holy Spirit living within you, you can have joy and peace. You no longer have to be controlled by life's ups and downs. You now have it within you to be in control of your attitude and reaction to every moment and event of every day!

That's what Jesus told his disciples on the last night before his death. Their world would present them with trouble, but they could have Jesus' joy and peace in the midst of it because of the indwelling Holy Spirit. His followers were about to begin experiencing a new, miraculous inner calm despite life's tribulations. The same Holy Spirit whom Jesus promised the disciples lives in you as well. You, too, can experience the daily hope Jesus promised them:

"I have told you this so that **my joy** may be in you and that your **joy** may be complete." (John 15:11 NIV)

"I have told you these things, so that in me you may have **peace**. In this world you will have trouble. But take heart! I have overcome the world." (John 16:33 NIV)

Experiencing Joy and Peace in Your Daily Life

"But the **Helper**, the **Holy Spirit**, whom the Father will send in my name, he will teach you all things and bring to your remembrance all that I have said to you." (John 14:26)

The translation above describes the Holy Spirit as Helper. Other translations of the Bible give the Holy Spirit different descriptive names such as Advocate, Counselor, and Comforter.

Let's briefly explore the wonderful promise of peace Jesus made to his disciples the night before he went to the cross:

"**Peace** I leave with you; **my peace** I give to you. Not as the world gives do I give to you. Let not your hearts be troubled, neither let them be afraid." (John 14:27)

Through your relationship with the Holy Spirit, you can have contentment in any situation. Far beyond being a mere coping mechanism, God the Father has placed the Holy Spirit within you to guide you through every situation of your life:

But the fruit of the Spirit is love, **joy, peace,** patience, kindness, goodness, faithfulness, gentleness, self-control; against such things there is no law. (Galatians 5:22–23)

The joy and peace Jesus spoke of on his last night before going to the cross is part of the fruit of the Holy Spirit. When you are walking in the Spirit, you will experience all of the fruit of the Spirit, including joy and peace. This joy and peace, which far surpasses the world's fickle happiness that ebbs and flows with life's uncontrollable circumstances, is available to you regardless of your situation.

Experiencing the Holy Spirit's Joy and Peace

Happiness comes from the external world, while joy comes from the indwelling Holy Spirit. Happiness comes and goes with your often unmanageable situations, while joy can flow from your relationship with Jesus in any situation.

> "Let not your hearts be troubled. Believe in God; believe also in me." (John 14:1)

Learning to trust Jesus and experience the power of the Holy Spirit takes practice. As you trust him in the minor details of ordinary days, you're preparing to trust him when life's bigger challenges arise. Yes, there will still be sadness and grief, but relying on his indwelling presence in the person of the Holy Spirit will bring you hope.

You become increasingly better at handling life's uncertainties, disappointments, and heartbreaks in ways that would otherwise be impossible. You develop the understanding that, through the Holy Spirit, you have the ability to persevere through circumstances you could never handle in your own strength.

What an exceptional blessing you have in the Holy Spirit!

You are the Permanent Residence of the Holy Spirit

On his last night before going to the cross, Jesus foreshadowed the coming of the Holy Spirit to the disciples. Amazingly, he said it would be better for him to leave so they could have the Helper—the Holy Spirit:

> "Nevertheless, I tell you the truth: it is to your advantage that I go away, for if I do not go away, **the Helper** will not come to you. But if I go, I will send him to you." (John 16:7)

Jesus said that since they had been *with him*, they had already experienced the presence of the Holy Spirit. And beginning at Pentecost, though Jesus would be gone from the earth, the Holy Spirit would now be *in them*. Jesus told them:

> "… the Spirit of truth. The world cannot accept him, because it neither sees him nor knows him. But you know him, for he lives with you and will be **in you.**" (John 14:17 NIV)

The same is true for you today. When God forgave your sins and saved you, you crossed over from death to life. You received the greatest gift of all, eternal life, when you were forgiven for your sins and became a child of God. At that moment, God the Father gave you a guarantee of eternal inheritance by placing the person of the Holy Spirit in your heart.

> When you believed, you were marked in him with a **seal,** the promised Holy Spirit, who is a deposit **guaranteeing** our inheritance until the redemption of those who are God's possession—to the praise of his glory. (Ephesians 1:13–14 NIV)

You were born again spiritually and received the person of the Holy Spirit to live in you forever. The Holy Spirit now dwells in you, which means he actually lives within you. He doesn't live in temples built by men, but has instead made your heart his permanent home. As we will explore further in chapter 10, you are now the very temple of the Holy Spirit.

> Do you not know that your body is a **temple** of the Holy Spirit **within** you, whom you have from God? You are not your own. (1 Corinthians 6:19)

Jesus promised the disciples, "And I will ask the Father, and he will give you another Helper, to be with you **forever**" (John 14:16). He said the Holy Spirit would indwell them *forever*. And the same is true for you!

The Holy Spirit doesn't come and go as he did in Old Testament times. He is always present and living within you, even when you sin. He's sealed you as a child of God, and guaranteed your salvation, regardless of your future actions. The Holy Spirit is your new spiritual DNA, and he will never leave you. He has come to lead, teach, comfort, and empower you. You are a new person, forever indwelt with the Holy Spirit of God.

> Therefore, if anyone is in Christ, he is a new creation. The old has passed away; behold, the new has come. (2 Corinthians 5:17)

After the dish-smashing incident I described at the beginning of the book, when Juli first said she could see a dramatic change in me, I began making it my first priority to walk in the Spirit. I experienced such a profound positive lift in my outlook on life that, on several occasions, I exclaimed to Juli, "I know this is bad theology, but I feel like I have been born again, *again!*" I was experiencing the fruit of the Spirit, including joy and peace, in a way I hadn't seen in my life since my first few days as a new believer ten years earlier.

My desire to read the Bible increased, and the Holy Spirit made its words come alive in new ways, just as he had a decade earlier when I was a new believer. My faith had a new freshness and my passions turned from the things of the world to the things of Jesus. That zeal made my conversations naturally turn to spiritual topics as well.

I had a sense of realization similar to Dorothy in *The Wizard of Oz*, when she understood the red slippers she had been wearing all along held the secret to what was important. All she had to do was click her heels to experience the life she wanted. Though the Holy Spirit had been living within me all along, I had never experienced the fullness of his joy and peace like I suddenly was!

God has given you the person of the Holy Spirit to help you live the life he has planned for you. You lack nothing you need to live a life pleasing to God now that you have received the Holy Spirit. The Bible says God "poured out" his Holy Spirit on you at the time of your salvation:

> But when the kindness and love of God our Savior appeared, he saved us, not because of righteous things we had done, but because of his mercy. He saved us through the washing of **rebirth and renewal by the Holy Spirit, whom he poured out on us generously** through Jesus Christ our Savior. (Titus 3:4–6 NIV)

God didn't give you the Holy Spirit just so you can be certain you are going to heaven when you die. He gave you the Holy Spirit so you can joyfully be a part of bringing heaven to earth while you live! What a supremely rich blessing God has given you in the person of the Holy Spirit! The key is to learn, by faith, the secrets of keeping in step with the Holy Spirit throughout each day.

What Spills Out When You Are Bumped?

My first mentor, Dr. Bert Harned, liked to ask, "When you get bumped, what spills out?" The lesson being that if you're operating in the flesh, when life's difficulties "bump" you, then anger, frustration, etc., will spill out. But if you are walking in the Spirit, the fruit of the Spirit will spill out.

Juli once illustrated this in a memorable example. We were taking our first trip together as newlyweds, driving along the Oregon coast for several days. We had very little on our agenda, allowing us to take our time and fully enjoy each other's company. One morning, we stopped and had breakfast along the highway where Juli ordered a latte to go. She savored a few sips, then we walked back to the car to resume our drive.

I first had to back onto a busy street, and, unfortunately, I was paying more attention to the traffic than to Juli. She had her latte in her left hand up high, and as I turned to look behind me, my elbow hit her latte, not only knocking the top off the cup but dumping almost the entire contents of the cup onto her head.

Juli ducked down, and I couldn't see her face. She was bent over for a of couple seconds with her hair drenched and latte dripping off her head, arm, and shoulder. I stopped and braced myself for what I assumed would be an unhappy reaction of some type. I mean, I had just drenched her in a hot, sticky drink! Who wouldn't be upset, right?

But to my surprise, after a couple of seconds she lifted her face and she was laughing so hard she could barely breathe. I was both stunned and relieved!

I suspect the vast majority of people would have been very upset. If Juli had been living in the flesh in Level II, even as good-natured as she is, she wouldn't have been able to suddenly control the natural, fleshly reaction of anger and instantly change her attitude to force herself to laugh. But because she was living by the power of the Holy Spirit at the moment she was bumped, her immediate reaction was joy, gentleness, goodness, and self-control.

When Juli was bumped and the latte spilled out *on* her, the fruit of the Spirit spilled *out* of her! What a great picture of how we look when we are empowered by the Holy Spirit and encounter a very difficult situation.

Not only did Juli have a Spirit-controlled initial reaction, but she chose to continue to walk in the Spirit for the rest of the day. We had all of our clothes packed in the trunk, no hotel room where we could get cleaned up, a two-hour drive ahead of us, and she had a sticky, fragrant latte all over her. Yet, remarkably, she handled that difficult situation with laughter! Her reaction wasn't a fleshly, angry, hostile reaction that created strife, but a gentle, kind, pleasant reaction that created harmony.

What a blessed man I am to be married to a woman who keeps in step with and lives by the power of the Holy Spirit.

We all need the power of the Holy Spirit for when life "spills a latte" on us. The majority of your life is not made up of big, dramatic experiences. It consists mostly of smaller daily events and little surprises, both good and bad. Life has its share of unexpected annoyances and disappointments. But if you are led by the Spirit, you can handle these undesirable events joyfully. The world is watching to see how you, as a follower of Jesus, react when life disappoints you.

Peace Surpassing Human Understanding

> The Lord is near. **Do not be anxious about anything,** but in every situation, by prayer and petition, with thanksgiving, present your requests to God. And the **peace of God, which transcends all understanding,** will guard your hearts and your minds in Christ Jesus. (Philippians 4:5–7 NIV)

These are the words the apostle Paul penned to the Philippian church while under house arrest and chained to a Roman guard. Despite his circumstances, he was filled with peace rather than anxiety because he had prayed and surrendered his life and its difficulties to God. He was not only instructing the Philippian church and us, but also giving us an example of how he was personally thriving in the midst of unjust imprisonment. He had an inner tranquility that was beyond human understanding.

Because you have within you the same Holy Spirit Paul had, that same tranquility is available to you today. It isn't just peace *from* God, it is the peace *of* God. The indwelling Spirit's peace is not always explainable, but it is always available to you as you ask God for it.

Your Life in the Spirit

The Bible describes your life with the Holy Spirit in many ways, such as being filled with the Spirit, walking in the Spirit, keeping in step with the Spirit, living in the Spirit, and others. They all mean the same thing—living by the power of the Holy Spirit and not our own, flawed flesh. They all result in experiencing and exhibiting the fruit of the Spirit.

Now that you have been indwelt by the Holy Spirit forever, the question constantly before you is: How much of the time are you living in the power and fullness of the Holy Spirit? That is, what percentage of the time are you living in the flesh in Level II, and what percentage of the time are you living as God intends you to live, in the power and presence of the Spirit in Level III?

The objective of the remainder of this book is to help you greatly increase the amount of time you live empowered by the Holy Spirit. God desires for you to live a life pleasing to him and influential to others. He wants your life to have meaning and purpose and has given you the Holy Spirit to guide, teach, and empower you in your journey!

※

ABIDING TRUTH

When you walk in the Spirit,
you will experience love, joy, and peace.

REFLECTION QUESTIONS

1. Many people mistake happiness for joy. What are the key differences between the two?

2. Who have you met in your life who seemed to be joyful regardless of their circumstances?

3. Consider when you've felt most peaceful with Christ. What was it about that time or circumstance that made you feel secure in him?

4. What are some of the ways you've already adopted to walk in the Spirit so you can experience more of the Holy Spirit's joy and peace? Why is it important for us as believers to build habits that push us to remember the Holy Spirit's presence? What new habits do you sense the Holy Spirit is giving you to begin?

5. John 16:33 says, "I have told you these things, so that in me you may have peace. In this world you will have trouble. But take heart! I have overcome the world" (NIV). How does this verse make you feel? Where do you usually experience peace? How can you carry this forward to make it real in your life as a follower of Jesus?

6. Take a moment to imagine what your life would look like if you were experiencing the full peace and joy offered by the Holy Spirit. Jot down one or two things that might be keeping you from experiencing this fruit. Pause for thirty seconds and pray that the Holy Spirit would work in and through you to remove these roadblocks, bringing you closer to him.

SONG SUGGESTIONS

"Peace Be Still" by The Belonging Co
"Safe" by Phil Wickham

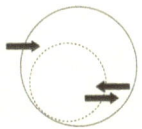

CHAPTER 5

The Power of the Holy Spirit

You may have read the story of Pentecost described in Acts 2 many times. For most followers of Jesus, much like Easter, we never tire of hearing about the miraculous, world-changing day of Pentecost that took place over 2,000 years ago. Everything was made new that day when the Holy Spirit was given by God to live in the hearts of each person who repented and put their faith in Jesus. On that day the church was born.

Let's look briefly at the days leading up to Pentecost.

After Jesus died on the cross and was resurrected from the dead, he appeared to the disciples and many others on earth for forty days. He walked, talked, and ate with them, leaving no doubt that he'd overcome death and was alive and living among them physically.

But his followers didn't know what to expect when Jesus told them to wait in Jerusalem and said: "But **you will receive power** when the Holy Spirit has come upon you" (Acts 1:8). Nevertheless, you can only imagine the sense of wonder and excitement they experienced when they heard Jesus' promise.

Then miraculously, he flew up into the clouds and out of sight. But unlike the discouragement they faced after Jesus' death on the cross, this time they stayed together, obediently waiting on the arrival of the promised Holy Spirit. This time when Jesus departed, his followers' waiting was completely different.

The first time Jesus departed he was dead (John 19:33). This time he was alive (John 20:14–18).

The first time he departed it looked as if death had won over him (Luke 23:46). This time everybody knew he had won over death (Luke 24:33–48).

The first time he departed it appeared Satan had won (Luke 22:53). This time it was obvious Satan had lost (1 John 3:8).

The first time he departed he went into the ground (Matthew 27:58–66). This time he flew into the sky (Acts 1:9).

The first time he departed he was placed in a tomb (Mark 15:46). This time God the Father placed him on the throne (Hebrews 10:12).

Therefore, knowing something special was on the horizon, Jesus' followers behaved in a completely different manner.

Instead of being hopeless (John 20:11–13), this time his followers were hopeful (John 20:19–20).

Instead of hiding because of their fear of others (John 20:19), this time they sang praises because of their great hope in God (Luke 24:53).

Instead of scattering (John 20:10), this time they stayed together and prayed, waiting for the arrival of the promised Holy Spirit (Acts 1:14).

They were not disappointed! Ten days later, as thousands gathered at the large Jewish festival called Pentecost, God sent his Holy Spirit, and the world and eternity were changed forever.

Pentecost

Here's a portion of the account of the day of Pentecost:

> When the day of Pentecost arrived, they were all together in one place. And suddenly there came from heaven a sound like a mighty rushing wind, and it filled the entire house where they were sitting. And divided tongues as of fire appeared to them and rested on each one of them. And they were all **filled with the Holy Spirit** and began to speak in other tongues as the Spirit gave them utterance. (Acts 2:1–4)

Then Peter, filled and empowered by the Holy Spirit, preached what was essentially the first sermon of the new church, concluding:

"This Jesus God raised up, and of that we all are witnesses. Being therefore exalted at the right hand of God, and having received from the Father the promise of the Holy Spirit, he has poured out this that you yourselves are seeing and hearing ... Let all the house of Israel therefore know for certain that God has made him both Lord and Christ, this Jesus whom you crucified." (Acts 2:32–36)

The account goes on to say:

Now when they heard this they were cut to the heart, and said to Peter and the rest of the apostles, "Brothers, what shall we do?" And Peter said to them, "Repent and be baptized every one of you in the name of Jesus Christ for the forgiveness of your sins, and you will receive the gift of the Holy Spirit. For the promise is for you and for your children and for all who are far off, everyone whom the Lord our God calls to himself." And with many other words he bore witness and continued to exhort them, saying, "Save yourselves from this crooked generation." So those who received his word were baptized, and there were added that day about three thousand souls. (vv. 37–41)

At Pentecost over 2,000 years ago, God sent his Holy Spirit into his followers' hearts in a one-time, dramatic display no one could miss, and that event has been recounted endlessly! While the filling of the Spirit isn't as dramatic today, the same power is nevertheless real, available, and just as life-changing.

The Great Provision of the Holy Spirit

Shortly before he ascended into heaven, Jesus gave his disciples two important messages. First, he gave them (and us) their marching orders on *what* they were to do after his departure in what has come to be known as the Great Commission:

"Go therefore and make disciples of all nations, baptizing them in the name of the Father and of the Son and of the Holy Spirit, teaching them to observe all that I have commanded you. And behold, I am with you always, to the end of the age." (Matthew 28:19–20)

Then, just a little later, Jesus told them *how* they were to carry it out. He instructed them to wait in the city of Jerusalem until they had received the person and the power of the Holy Spirit.

"And behold, I am sending the promise of my Father upon you. But stay in the city until **you are clothed with power from on high.**" (Luke 24:49)

"But you will receive power when the Holy Spirit has come upon you, and you will be my witnesses in Jerusalem and in all Judea and Samaria, and to the end of the earth." (Acts 1:8)

We'll call the gift of the Holy Spirit indwelling us the Great Provision. The Great Commission of Jesus had to wait on the Great Provision of the Holy Spirit. God gave the Great Provision of the Holy Spirit who lives in the heart *of* every follower of Jesus to carry out the Great Commission that is a command *to* every follower of Jesus. God's plan is to use people as his witnesses throughout the world by the power of the Holy Spirit.

The Great Provision of the Holy Spirit enables the Great Commission of Jesus. This was true with the birth of the church at Pentecost and has continued to be true throughout history right up to today. We are able to carry out the Great Commission because *we* are not doing the witnessing and teaching. Rather, *it's the Holy Spirit living in and through us.* What God commands, he empowers through the Great Provision of the person and power of the Holy Spirit.

Dynamic Power

I'm certainly not a Biblical scholar, and when somebody tells me the original Greek word for a word in the Bible, I typically cannot remember it.

But here's a Greek word I can remember and find helpful, and I think you'll find it helpful too. It's the Greek word *dunamis*, (pronounced **doo-nam-is**), which means *power*. This is the word Jesus used when he told of the power of the Holy Spirit. It's the same word from which we get our English word *dynamite*.

As a follower of Jesus, you have inside you the dynamic power of the Holy Spirit. But that power needs to be triggered by a spark. The spark that sets off the explosion of the dynamic power of the Holy Spirit within you is *faith*.

Without faith your power is dormant—almost as if it doesn't exist. As seen in the chocolate milk video on abidingroom.com, followers of Jesus in whom the power lies dormant have lives that look pretty much the same as the lives of unbelievers; that is until the spark of faith ignites the power of the Holy Spirit and unleashes the potential God has planned for them. We'll explore the importance of faith in greater detail in chapter 16.

Obedience Keeps the Power Flowing

After that spark has been ignited and you are living empowered by the Holy Spirit, you continue to stay empowered by obedience. Obedience maintains your living in the Spirit. Disobedience, on the other hand, causes what the Bible calls "quenching the Spirit."

Do not quench the Spirit. (1 Thessalonians 5:19)

Just as we can choose to live by the Spirit and not sin, we can choose instead to live by our no-good flesh and sin. When we sin, we quench the power of the Holy Spirit. Because God is love, no sin can expel the permanent presence of the Holy Spirit. But when we choose to sin, we extinguish the Holy Spirit's full power in our lives. In chapter 3, we saw that our sin *grieves* the *person* of the Holy Spirit. Now we see that our sin also *quenches* the *power* of the Holy Spirit.

About a year after my dish-smashing incident in 1999, I experienced in a very memorable way how obedience can reveal the power of the Holy Spirit. I sensed God leading me to take a personal day of rest—a personal

Sabbath—every two weeks. He laid on my heart that he was instructing me to take the day to unplug from work and simply spend time with Jesus.

In our office at that point, I handled all the client calls that involved investment and tax recommendations, which was generally about ten calls a day. These calls often required quick action, so it was a little scary to miss them. Though my staff of four was certainly competent in their duties, none were qualified to handle these calls.

But since I knew the Holy Spirit was leading me to do this, I chose to operate by faith and begin taking a personal Sabbath day.

I took a deep breath and explained to my staff that God was leading me to do this and took my first day off. Generally, I evaluate the success of any day by the number and importance of things I can check off my to-do list. However, on this day, I attempted to do the opposite of what I normally did. I put away my phone and any type of agenda, listened to some sermons and Christian music, took some walks, rested, and tried to listen to what the Holy Spirit was saying to me. It was wonderfully restful.

As I went to work the next day, I was a bit apprehensive to see what had occurred the previous day. I went to my desk expecting to see at least ten phone messages I needed to address, but I found none. I went to the receptionist and asked her for my calls, and surprisingly, she said I didn't have any. I was somewhat in disbelief, so I asked her to verify what she'd just told me. She repeated that the phone hadn't rung at all the previous day. I was puzzled, as I'm sure my staff was, but I was also quite thankful it had been a quiet day.

Two weeks later, it was again time to take my personal Sabbath. I took another deep breath and took the day off. The following morning, I came back into the office and when I arrived at my desk to look for the messages, once again there weren't any. By the time I went to the front desk, the rest of the staff was waiting there too. I asked the receptionist where my messages were, and she told me the phones hadn't rung once while I was away. As far as I could recall, in the twelve years since we had opened our office, we had never had a day where we didn't get a few calls.

Two weeks later, on the day after my third personal Sabbath day, when I arrived at the office, all four of the staff people were gathered around the front desk waiting for me. They were all silently looking at me with big eyes of anticipation and were smiling at me as I walked in.

"Let me guess," I said. "The phones didn't ring at all."

One of them exclaimed excitedly, "This is the weirdest thing. It's like everyone knows you're gone. The phones didn't ring once!"

We all knew something beyond coincidence was occurring, and I shared what I knew to be true—God was teaching us *he* owned the business and had it all under control. He was also teaching us that when he puts something on our hearts to do, we need to be obedient and trust him.

When we trust God and are obedient to do what he's instructing us to do, he will send his Helper to come alongside us. Not only do we get to see him work in our lives, but other people—many of them who aren't following the Lord—will also get to see him at work in undeniable ways.

Empowered Living

What does a Spirit-empowered life look like? Let's look at four purposes of the power of the Holy Spirit in your life:

1. Power for daily living
2. Power to keep God's commands
3. Power over sin
4. Power to share your faith

Power for Daily Living

Through the Holy Spirit, God has given you the ability to handle life's difficulties in a godly manner. When you harness the power of the Holy Spirit, you have the power to control your tongue. You have the power to control your anger. You have the self-control to resist temptation. You are able to be gentle when others are harsh to you. You can be kind when others mistreat you. You can be patient toward others. The Holy Spirit gives you the power to genuinely love disagreeable, nasty people.

You are even able to laugh when your spouse bumps you and your coffee spills all over your head!

The Bible confirms that when you live by the power of the Holy Spirit, you have capabilities you wouldn't otherwise have.

> For God gave us a spirit not of fear but of power and love and self-control. (2 Timothy 1:7)

And in John 15, Jesus says it is impossible to live the Christian life apart from him. That means it is also impossible to live it apart from the empowerment of the Helper, the Holy Spirit.

While you can trust the Holy Spirit to empower you for daily living, there is no evidence in the Bible that says when you are living by the Spirit your life will be one continuous string of phenomenal, emotional experiences. These experiences are wonderful when they occur, but they are the exception, not the norm. Life in the Spirit doesn't mean freedom from problems, it means power to live with them in a new way.

Thankfully, the power of the Holy Spirit is available to you every minute of every day! By accessing the power of the Holy Spirit within you, you can live through difficult circumstances and handle tough problems with tranquility. Because you are indwelt by the Holy Spirit, each one of the fruit of the Spirit is available to you throughout your day.

It's a matter of choosing to live each moment by the Spirit and not the flesh. With practice, over time, these choices become a normal part of your new way of living. Day by day, as you live by the power of the Holy Spirit, God is continually developing greater Christlike character in you.

Power to Keep God's Commands

Jesus told the disciples that when the Holy Spirit came to live within them, they would receive power (Luke 24:49; Acts 1:8). This includes the power to obey biblical commands. When you are filled with and led by the person of the Holy Spirit, he empowers you to carry out the commands found in the Bible.

Only by the power of the Holy Spirit are we able to be obedient to biblical instruction, such as for all of us to honor our mothers and fathers (Exodus 20:12), for husbands to love their wives as Christ loved the church (Ephesians 5:25), and for fathers to not exasperate their children (Ephesians 6:4). We're able to live out what is referred to as the Golden Rule—to do to others as you would have them do to you (Matthew 7:12).

The Holy Spirit gives you the power to obey challenging commands such as love others as Christ has loved you (John 13:34), forgive as God has forgiven you (Colossians 3:13), and love your enemies (Matthew 5:44).

When you see that challenging list, does it make you feel as if you need some help with those commands? I certainly do! But thankfully, when we are filled, led, and empowered by the Holy Spirit, he enables us to live them out. God never commands anything he doesn't enable through the power of the Holy Spirit.

Power Over Sin

> For the law of **the Spirit of life has set you free** in Christ Jesus **from the law of sin** and death. For God has done what the law, weakened by the flesh, could not do. By sending his own Son in the likeness of sinful flesh and for sin, he condemned sin in the flesh, **in order that the righteous requirement** of the law **might be fulfilled in us, who walk** not according to the flesh but **according to the Spirit.** (Romans 8:2–4)

Using only the words shown in bold above, let's piece together God's Word, assuring you that you have power over sin:

"The Spirit of life has set you free … from the law of sin … in order that the righteous requirement … might be fulfilled in us, who walk … according to the Spirit."

Part of the fruit of the Spirit is self-control. Self-control gives you the ability to not sin. You now have the power to do the right thing and not the wrong thing. Any persistent sin that seems to have control over you absolutely does not! You were given power over that sin when you were given the Holy Spirit. It is a matter of appropriating the power you have already been given.

> So you also must consider yourselves **dead to sin and alive to God in Christ Jesus.** Let not sin therefore reign in your mortal body, to make you obey its passions. Do not present your members to sin as instruments for unrighteousness, but present yourselves

to God as those who have been brought from death to life, and your members to God as instruments for righteousness. **For sin will have no dominion over you,** since you are not under law but under grace. (Romans 6:11–14)

When you became a believer in Jesus, you became a new creation. You received new desires to do good and to please God. Along with these new desires, God also gave you the Holy Spirit who enables you to live a righteous life. The Holy Spirit gives you both the will and the power to not sin.

The minority of Christians who live most of each day in the power of the Holy Spirit know the refreshing reality of seeing sin that used to rule their lives now be overcome by living by the Spirit. And that is exactly what God desires for you and why he has given you the Holy Spirit to enable you to live out the life he has planned for you!

Power to Share Your Faith

In spite of the many missteps the disciples made during the three years they had been with him, Jesus told them that through the power of the Holy Spirit they would become effective witnesses for his name not only locally but throughout the world.

> "But you will receive power when the Holy Spirit has come upon you, and **you will be my witnesses** in Jerusalem and in all Judea and Samaria, and to the end of the earth." (Acts 1:8)

You have received the same Holy Spirit the disciples received. God didn't give you the Holy Spirit so you can use God for *your* purposes; he gave you the Holy Spirit so he can empower you for *his* purposes. Just like the disciples, you can't do this by your own strategy or ingenuity. But as you let the Holy Spirit guide and empower your words and actions, you can be an effective witness for Jesus too.

The Power of the Holy Spirit

Power for Everything You Need

We have just seen that God has made some remarkable promises to you in the Bible. By faith in Jesus and by the power of the Holy Spirit, you can experience the life God has planned for you. The apostle Peter sums it up by reminding us God has graciously given you power for everything you need to live a godly life.

> His divine **power has given us everything we need** for a godly life through our knowledge of him who called us by his own glory and goodness. (2 Peter 1:3 NIV)

ABIDING TRUTH

As a follower of Jesus, you are indwelt by the Holy Spirit. He gives you the power to carry out God's commands and live a life of freedom from sin.

REFLECTION QUESTIONS

1. How can you explain to a new believer how the power of the Holy Spirit works? What are some of the questions you still have about this?

2. Based on your experience and understanding, as well as what you've learned in this book, take a moment to write a brief description of the Holy Spirit.

3. Based on what has been discussed in this book, what differences are there between the power of the Holy Spirit in the Old Testament versus his power in the New Testament? Why might it be important to know those differences as a Christian today?

4. Understanding the availability of the Spirit's power is the first part of being able to access that power regularly. What are some of the ways you could (or already do) align yourself with the Holy Spirit to maximize the flow of his power?

5. Why is it so important for us to rely on the Holy Spirit's power to do God's work? What do you suppose God is trying to develop in us when we align with the Spirit?

SONG SUGGESTIONS

"Same Power" by Jeremy Camp
"Whom Shall I Fear [The God of Angel Armies]" by Chris Tomlin
"God of Wonders" by Mac Powell, with Cliff and Danielle Young

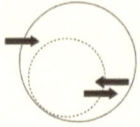

CHAPTER 6

Be Filled with the Spirit

Be filled with the Spirit. (Ephesians 5:18)

As we learned in chapter 5, the arrival of the Holy Spirit in the hearts of believers changed everything. As a follower of Jesus, the Holy Spirit indwells you. That is, he lives inside you. Your loving heavenly Father has placed his Spirit in you to accompany you everywhere, guiding you and empowering you to live a life pleasing to him.

The distinguishing characteristic of you as a follower of Jesus is the indwelling presence of the Holy Spirit. It's not a question of *if* you have the Holy Spirit—all followers of Jesus do. It's also not a question of *how much* of the Holy Spirit you have—all followers of Jesus have the entire person of the Holy Spirit. The real question is *how much of you* does the Holy Spirit have? Are you *filled* with the Spirit?

In the book of Acts, believers in the early church are consistently described as being "filled with the Spirit." In letters to the early churches, Paul instructs them to live Spirit-filled lives by using terms such as "walk in the Spirit," "led by the Spirit," "live by the Spirit," "keep in step with the Spirit," and "be filled with the Spirit." Each of these terms instructs believers to operate by the power of the Holy Spirit, not the flesh. Each phrase has a similar meaning and intent—the Holy Spirit (and not your flesh) is leading you.

We've seen the Bible clearly illustrates The 3 Levels of Life. When you're filled with the Spirit, you're in the Abiding Room, where you're living a Level III life, as the next diagram reminds us.

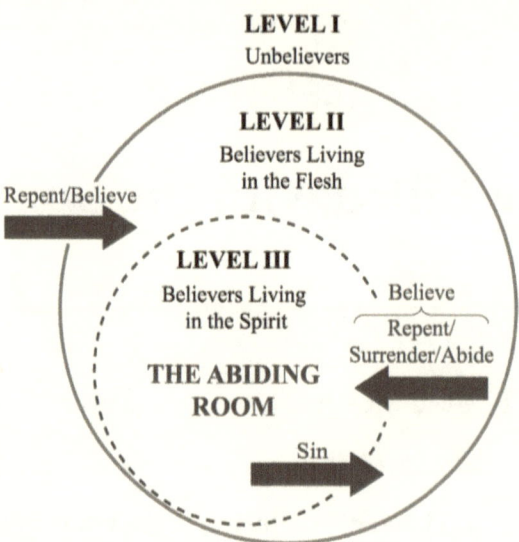

God's Temple

In the Old Testament, God's Spirit lived among his people in a tabernacle, or temple. Today that temple is no longer a man-made structure. Now the new temple housing God's Holy Spirit is *you!*

> Do you not know that **your bodies are temples of the Holy Spirit,** who is in you, whom you have received from God? You are not your own; you were bought at a price. Therefore honor God with your bodies. (1 Corinthians 6:19–20 NIV)

Every follower of Jesus is the temple of God and indwelt with the person of the Holy Spirit. It's God's desire that you, your body, and your life put his glory on display. This is accomplished when you are filled with his Spirit.

You never have to be concerned the Holy Spirit might leave you. He has made you his permanent home. It is true that when you sin, because God is holy, the Holy Spirit is grieved (Ephesians 4:30) and his power quenched (1 Thessalonians 5:19). Nevertheless, because God is love, his Spirit will not depart. You were saved once and forever because God is *love*, but you are constantly being refined because he is *holy*.

Be Filled with the Spirit

What does it mean to "be filled with the Spirit"?

1. *"Be filled" is a command.* You are commanded to be filled with the Spirit. But while you are commanded to be *filled* with the Spirit, you are never commanded to be *indwelt* with the Spirit. When used in reference to the Holy Spirit, the words "filled" and "indwelt" are not synonymous. That's because all believers are permanently indwelt with the Spirit at salvation, but are not permanently filled with the Spirit. The question is not whether you're indwelt with the Holy Spirit, but whether you're filled with the Holy Spirit at any given moment.
2. *The filling is an ongoing process.* "Be filled" actually means "be, being, continuously filled." It is not a one-time event, but rather an ongoing, moment-by-moment experience throughout our lives. The filling of the Holy Spirit enables our obedience to God's commands. And as we will see again later, as we continue to be obedient to what the Spirit prompts us to do, we continue to be filled with the Spirit. Continued obedience maintains the continuous filling. We're indwelt by the Holy Spirit once at salvation, but we need to be filled with the Spirit continually.

    On more than one occasion after presenting the chocolate milk illustration, someone has come up to me afterward with a grin saying I should stir in powdered chocolate that settles at the bottom over time. I agree—we tend to settle to our flesh and all need to be continuously stirred up!
3. *Being filled with the Spirit brings an experiential understanding of the phrase itself.* Jesus told the disciples they would receive the Holy Spirit, but they had to experience it to understand it. In fact, the book of Acts is one surprising life lesson after another to the early church of what the abiding, Spirit-filled life entails.

Many in the early church had never seen Jesus face-to-face, and they didn't have the Bible to read, but their Spirit-filled lives were writing it!

They had received minimal teaching about the Holy Spirit coming to indwell them, but the new believers knew without a doubt they were filled with him. Each account of the Spirit's work in the early church told in the book of Acts serves as a reminder that a personal experience *of* the Holy Spirit is the best teacher *about* the Holy Spirit.

God desires for you to experience him personally, not just academically or intellectually. While we now have the Bible to guide us and explain the role of the Holy Spirit, there's still no substitute for personally experiencing the Spirit to give us a fuller understanding of the biblical instructions themselves. The more you're obedient to biblical instructions, the more you'll experience the Holy Spirit in your life. That will, in turn, give you greater insight into the instructions' meaning. Obedience keeps us "stirred up!"

Many Fillings of the Spirit

I have found it's not uncommon for followers of Jesus to incorrectly believe they are always filled with the Spirit. As mentioned earlier, we are always indwelt, but not always filled with the Spirit.

Here's an example of what is implied when Paul says, "Be filled with the Spirit." Let's say you drop your kids off at someone's house. You say to your kids, "Be good." When you say, "Be good," it implies you know they can also choose to be bad. You wouldn't say, "Be good," if they were always good.

Likewise, Paul wouldn't say, "Be filled with the Spirit," if the *only* option was to be filled with the Spirit. He's talking to followers of Jesus in the church of Ephesus who already have the Holy Spirit, so he isn't imploring unbelievers to be saved. He's instructing the believers to be continuously filled with the Spirit. Therefore, we can conclude followers of Jesus are *not always* filled with the Spirit. The presence of the Holy Spirit is permanent and unconditional, but the filling and the fullness of his power are conditional upon our life choices.

Let's look at another example. Let's say you're blue-eyed. If I say to you, "Be blue-eyed," you would understandably respond, "That's silly. I'm already blue-eyed, and that's the only thing I can be." Similarly, just as we wouldn't say to a blue-eyed person, "Be blue-eyed," Paul wouldn't say, "Be filled with the Spirit," if the *only* thing we as believers can be is filled with the Spirit. His exhortation to be filled implies followers of Jesus are *not always* filled with the Holy Spirit. Again, the filling of the Holy Spirit in your life is a continuous process you as a believer need to continually seek. You had one salvation, but you're instructed to seek many, continuous fillings.

As we discussed previously, the words and diagrams we're using to describe our relationship with the Holy Spirit have limitations. Is a person we've described as "filled with the Spirit" absolutely 100 percent filled with the Spirit, but a person who is 99 percent led by the Spirit, not filled with the Spirit? No, it is simply a way to describe whether we're living primarily in the Spirit or the flesh.

Yet, the Bible doesn't mince words by saying, "Be partially filled," or "Be almost filled." It's another statement made in absolutes to emphasize the point that the matter at hand is critical. In situations where we use the phrase "be filled with the Spirit," we might also say, "be continuously, *predominantly* filled, led, and empowered by the Holy Spirit." Don't get tangled up in the semantics of the words, but rather be inspired by their promises for your life!

Surprised By the Spirit

A few weeks after I had my dish-smashing incident, Juli noticed a significant difference in me. She noticed I was unusually gentle and kind, which is evidence of the fruit of the Spirit. But when she informed me she'd seen a change, I was completely unaware of it.

It is worth noting I:

- did not notice I was being kind and gentle
- did not have an emotional experience
- did not ask to be filled with the Spirit
- did not know I was filled with the Spirit

Even after I'd been informed of a change, which had been very apparent to Juli for several days, and despite being in church my entire life, I did not understand what had occurred. It took a couple weeks of reading the Bible before God revealed what had happened to me.

One morning, while reading Romans 7 and 8, the Holy Spirit showed me I had gone from living in the flesh to living by the power of the Holy Spirit. Even after I became aware of what had happened, I wasn't immediately sure how to "keep it going." It was exciting, but still pretty overwhelming and mysterious.

Importantly, there's no connection between the filling of the Spirit and your biblical head knowledge or the length of time you've been following Jesus. A head full of knowledge isn't the prerequisite for having a humble heart filled with the Spirit. God has no trouble finding and filling your fully surrendered heart!

It is the emptying of the heart of self that cleanses the temple for the filling of the Spirit. The first group of believers who were filled with the Spirit at Pentecost had very little idea of what was about to happen. They were just ordinary people obediently praying while they waited on God for the promised Holy Spirit.

God wants to fill you with his Spirit even more than you want to be filled. He already knows how he is going to use you for his kingdom purposes when you are fully empowered for his glory. If you take care of the preparation, God will take care of the visitation!

Your Life Is Your Ministry

Did you know you have an important ministry right now? You may not have a formal ministry with an official name, but if you're a follower of Jesus, you've already been given a ministry. The world is watching you and the character you display. The most significant ministry anyone can have is to lead a life empowered by the Holy Spirit that is seen by a watching world as they go about their day-to-day activities.

Today, when you walk out the front door and encounter people, make no mistake, you are bearing witness to Jesus. Will your witness be of a person walking in the Spirit or in the flesh? People are watching you and drawing conclusions from your life about who Jesus is. It's not a question of *if* your life will bear witness as to who Jesus is; the real question is *what type* of witness you will bear. Will it be your *fleshly* character or the *Christlike* character of Jesus?

When you're living out the Spirit-filled life and exhibiting the fruit of the Spirit, who does that look like? Jesus! The integrity and character of Jesus that was so attractive to you when you first believed becomes noticeable to others because it's actually Jesus they are seeing through your life! Isn't that remarkable?

Jesus promised his disciples the Holy Spirit would speak to them. In John 16:15 he said, "All that the Father has is mine; therefore I said that he [the Holy Spirit] will take what is mine and **declare it to you.**" That promise is still true today.

One of my experiences of hearing the Holy Spirit speak involves my parents' cabin a little over two hours away from our home in the Phoenix area. One night while sleeping at home, I woke up and, although I didn't hear it audibly, I sensed the Holy Spirit saying, "Go to the cabin." Well, I didn't want to drive all that way when I had no specific reason to go there, so I ignored the prompting and went back to sleep.

I woke up the next night and again sensed the Holy Spirit saying, "Go to the cabin." Again, I was unwilling to obey.

In the middle of the third night, I definitely heard, though not audibly, a very clear voice I knew was the Holy Spirit prompting me even more emphatically, "Go to the cabin!" It was so real and certain that I said aloud, "Okay!"

At 4:00 a.m., I informed my wife I was going to go to the cabin and took off. To prepare for what I expected to be an embarrassing situation, I began formulating stories in my mind as to what I was going to tell others as to why I drove to the cabin and found nothing wrong.

When I arrived at their cabin and opened the door, I was stunned to find water dripping through the ceiling into the kitchen from the upstairs, and the kitchen floor was flooded. As I walked in and looked down the hallway to the bedroom, I could see the ceiling had collapsed, and water had soaked everything. It was apparent the water had been running for a few days. Eventually I found the problem—the upstairs plumbing had sprung a small leak underneath the sink and was spraying a steady stream of water.

Recognizing when it's the Holy Spirit speaking and when it's just our imagination takes a lifetime of practice. We will never fully get it right in this life, but in this instance, I learned a good lesson about obeying immediately when I hear a firm prompting. If I had obeyed when I first heard it, the damage would have been far less, but it took three promptings from the Holy Spirit to get me to go. As others have said, "Delayed obedience is disobedience."

Fortunately, I did ultimately obey. I'm grateful God's Holy Spirit graciously spoke to me and prevented devasting damage, as there were no plans for anyone to go up to the cabin for another four weeks. There's no question the cabin would have been ruined.

The Blessings of the Spirit-Filled Life

Being filled with the Spirit means you are experiencing the joy of confidently resting in submission to the ongoing direction of the Holy Spirit. When you're filled with the Spirit, you have a greater ability to both know God's will and have the power to carry it out. The commands he's given you are meant to be carried out by the power of the Holy Spirit—not by you living in your own strength.

You can have peace in the midst of turmoil. You can have joy when things go wrong. You can experience inner stability in times of instability. When you are filled, led, and empowered by the Holy Spirit, you can live in a way that distinguishes you from the world because it is the Holy Spirit, not you, who is at work in and through you.

When you're filled with the Spirit, you will experience the blessings described in the three previous chapters on the Holy Spirit:

- You will exhibit the fruit of the Spirit, not the flesh.
- You will experience joy and peace in your life.
- You will receive power for daily living—power to keep God's commands, power to not sin, and power to share your faith.

Most importantly, you will bring glory and attention to God! How extraordinary and desirable does that sound?

All of this should lead you to ask another question: *"How* can I be continuously filled with the Spirit?" We'll answer that question in the next chapter: "The Great 2 for 1."

※

ABIDING TRUTH

As a follower of Jesus, you are always indwelt with the Spirit. And as you are obedient, you will be filled with the Spirit.

REFLECTION QUESTIONS

1. Any vehicle on the market today requires gasoline, electricity, or a combination of those fuel sources to function. The Holy Spirit is our fuel source. Why do you think God made us to need his power through the Holy Spirit? Why do you think he made us with the need to be filled regularly?

2. Consider the difference between being filled once and being filled as an ongoing process. How does this reality impact your daily living?

3. What are some of your favorite ways to realize this filling of the Spirit in your life? (Don't read too much into this question—all answers are applicable!)

4. Based on what you've already learned about the ways the Holy Spirit works in our lives, what are you doing that could hinder your being filled? What might you do to identify and eliminate these limitations?

5. What would you say to someone who told you they don't think they've ever been filled with the Holy Spirit? How would you help them understand this concept at a deeper level?

SONG SUGGESTIONS

"Fullness" by Elevation Worship
"Presence (My Heart's Desire)" by Newsboys

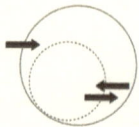

Part Three

THE ABIDING LIFE

CHAPTER 7

The Great 2 for 1

The purpose of this chapter is to explain the important connection between being *filled with the Holy Spirit*, which we explored in the previous chapter, and *abiding in Jesus*, which we will consider in the next two chapters.

To find a significant portion of Jesus' teaching on the abiding, Spirit-filled life, we can look at the end of his ministry on the night before he went to the cross. This Bible passage includes what is commonly known as the Last Supper. The apostle John tells us about it in his gospel, the book of John, in chapters 13 through 17. For the first time, Jesus laid out both how the Holy Spirit was about to be given to his disciples, as well as a new way to live—abiding in him.

As the evening begins, the disciples and Jesus are about to sit down for the Last Supper, and the disciples are talking among themselves. After three years of Jesus teaching them they should be humble, meek, and servant-hearted rather than promoting themselves, what are the disciples doing? Arguing about who among them is the greatest (Luke 22:24–30).

Jesus starts their time together with a new command, "Love one another."

> "A new command I give you: Love one another. As I have loved you, so you must love one another. By this everyone will know that you are my disciples, if you love one another." (John 13:34–35 NIV)

He then shows them an example of what love looks like by washing their feet.

Maybe we should give the disciples a little credit. At least they *believed* Jesus was the Messiah sent by God the Father, and they *knew* they were onto something big. That's why they had left everything to follow Jesus—to be part of the next big thing. That's why they were arguing over who was going to be at the top of this movement they believed was about to take off—they were gripped by selfish ambition.

Actually, they were underestimating the impact Jesus was about to have on time, heaven, earth, and eternity. They were still thinking in terms of merely an earthly kingdom. They didn't understand they were part of the biggest events in human history—Jesus going to the cross to die for the sin of humanity, rising from the dead, and sending the Holy Spirit to indwell them. They didn't understand this was to be the birth of the church.

The Foreshadowing of the Abiding, Spirit-Filled Life

It is very likely Jesus didn't tell his guys about the abiding, Spirit-filled life until the last night at dinner because they wouldn't be able to grasp it until they experienced it. And that wouldn't happen for another fifty-three days, when the Holy Spirit came in fullness within them at Pentecost.

But even though the disciples were unable to comprehend what was coming, Jesus gave them a sneak peek at the Last Supper. Previewing the coming of the abiding, Spirit-filled life at Pentecost, Jesus said:

> "I have told you now before it happens, so that when it does happen, you will believe." (John 14:29 NIV)

Both then and now, the abiding, Sprit-filled life must be experienced to be believed!

Love, Joy, and Peace

As we examine Jesus' last night before the cross, we'll see abiding in Jesus (remaining in constant fellowship with him) is what *also* brings about the filling of the Holy Spirit.

Chapters 13 through 17 comprise only 25 percent of the book of John. But by my count, 75 percent of the time John uses the words "love," "joy," and "peace" in his gospel is within these five chapters. Why are these chapters so packed with these three words? Because love, joy, and peace are fruit of the Holy Spirit.

When Jesus began foreshadowing the abiding, Spirit-filled life to his guys on that last night, he naturally talked about part of its blessing—love, joy, and peace. These fruit of the Spirit are evidence of the presence of the work of the Holy Spirit in the lives of Jesus' followers, both then and today.

The Great 2 for 1

In upcoming chapters, we'll explore in greater depth the reality that two very important commands regarding the abiding, Spirit-filled life are wonderfully connected. These two commands are Jesus saying, "Abide in me" (John 15:4), and the apostle Paul instructing us to "be filled with the Spirit" (Ephesians 5:18).

What is seldom understood is that when we are obedient to the first command to abide, Jesus completes our obedience to the second command to be filled as well. And he does this without any effort on our part! This means we are doubly blessed. The promise of the blessings of both abiding in Jesus and walking in the power of the Holy Spirit flows from simply remaining connected to Jesus. As we abide in Jesus, we are also being filled with the Holy Spirit.

In his book, *The Holy Spirit: Activating God's Power in Your Life*, the late, world-famous, evangelist Billy Graham wrote, "We are being filled as we abide in Christ."[1]

Abiding in Jesus and being filled with the Spirit are like different sides of the same coin. Just as a coin always has both "heads" and "tails," when you abide in Jesus, you always get filled with the Spirit.

Therefore, abiding in Jesus and being filled with the Spirit are linked, essentially forming a two for one spiritual reality available to us at all times. We will call this The Great 2 for 1.

Further Evidence of The Great 2 for 1

Let's take a further look at the relationship between abiding in Jesus and being filled with the Spirit from two perspectives: (1) continuous nature, and (2) active versus passive nature.

Continuous Nature: Abiding in Jesus and being filled with the Spirit are similar in that both are continuous. Abiding means remaining in constant fellowship with Jesus. It is not permanent but rather an ongoing obedience.

Likewise, as we have already seen, being filled with the Spirit is not permanent, but also the result of ongoing obedience. So, both abiding in Jesus and being filled with the Spirit are to be maintained through our ongoing, moment-to-moment obedience.

Active versus Passive Nature: Abiding in Jesus and being filled with the Spirit are different in that abiding is active while being filled is passive. Abiding is the active part we do. When Jesus says, *"Abide in me,"* he's instructing us to take action. It's our choice to engage in ongoing fellowship with Jesus.

On the other hand, being filled with the Spirit is passive. It is done for us by God as a result of our obedience to abide in Jesus. Being filled with the Spirit occurs quietly and effortlessly as we abide in Jesus. As we abide in him, the life of Jesus (the vine) flows into us (the branches) through his Holy Spirit. We will consider this further in the next two chapters on abiding in Jesus.

The command, "Be filled," gives us a hint of its passive nature by what it does *not* say. It does not say "Fill yourself with the Spirit." The instructions to be filled with the Spirit imply you are to do something, but you do not directly fill yourself with the Spirit. Instead, you *receive* the filling from God. It is not *accomplished* by you. Similar to how Jesus told the disciples they would *receive* power when they received the Holy Spirit, you, too, *receive* the filling again and again from God, but not of your own independent works.

We know, however, that since we are instructed to be filled, some type of action on our part is required that both precedes and results in our receiving the filling of the Spirit.

Abiding is the continuous action we do, while the filling of the Holy Spirit is the resulting continuous action God does as we abide. As we continuously choose to remain in fellowship with Jesus, we are continuously being filled with the Spirit.

Again, this is The Great 2 for 1.

Internal Fruit of Abiding—Love, Joy, and Peace

"As the Father has loved me, so have **I loved you. Abide in my love.** If you keep my commandments, you will **abide in my love**, just as I have kept my Father's commandments and **abide in his love**. These things I have spoken to you, that **my joy** may be in you, and that **your joy** may be full." (John 15:9–11)

"I have said these things to you, that in me you may have **peace**. In the world you will have tribulation. But take heart; I have overcome the world." (John 16:33)

Note the internal fruit and blessings of abiding are also the fruit of the Spirit—love, joy, and peace. That's why chapters 13 through 17 of the book of John, where Jesus introduces both abiding in him and the Holy Spirit, are packed full of words such as "love," "joy," and "peace." This again confirms The Great 2 for 1.

As we abide in Jesus, we are being filled with the Spirit, as evidenced by our love, joy, and peace. We're living Level III lives. We're in the Abiding Room.

In the next two chapters, we'll explore what Jesus means when he says, *"Abide in me."*

※

ABIDING TRUTH

The Great 2 for 1:
As you abide in Jesus,
you are being filled with the Holy Spirit.

REFLECTION QUESTIONS

1. How would you describe The Great 2 for 1 in your own words? What evidence is there that these two spiritual truths are linked? Why is this significant?

2. Do you agree if you are not abiding in Jesus, you cannot be filled with the Holy Spirit? Why or why not?

3. Having just studied the spiritual realties of walking in the Spirit, how does the connection between the Holy Spirit and abiding in Jesus impact your thinking as you prepare to examine the topic of abiding in Jesus in the next chapter?

SONG SUGGESTIONS

"In This Room" by We Are Compass Worship
"By Your Side" by Tenth Avenue North

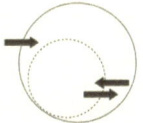

CHAPTER 8

The Vine and the Branches

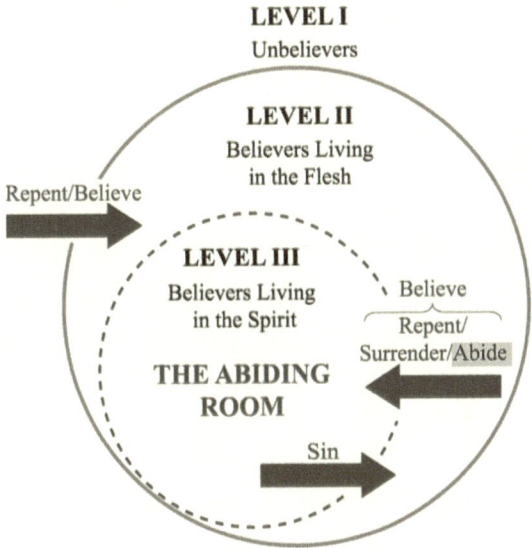

The diagram above is the primary Abiding Room diagram, with one small addition—the word "Abide" is shaded. As we continue to revisit this diagram, the subject of the discussion will be shaded for additional focus.

What does it mean to abide? First, let's look at what Jesus said about the significance of abiding in him.

"I am the true vine, and my Father is the vinedresser. Every branch in me that does not bear fruit he takes away, and every branch that does bear fruit he prunes, that it may bear more fruit. Already you are clean because of the word that I have spoken to you. Abide in me, and I in you. As the branch cannot bear fruit by itself, unless it abides in the vine, neither can you, unless you abide in me. I am the vine; you are the branches. Whoever abides in me and I in him, he it is that bears much fruit, for apart from me you can do nothing. If anyone does not abide in me he is thrown away like a branch and withers; and the branches are gathered, thrown into the fire, and burned. If you abide in me, and my words abide in you, ask whatever you wish, and it will be done for you. By this my Father is glorified, that you bear much fruit and so prove to be my disciples." (John 15:1–8)

Overview of Abiding

In John 15, Jesus introduces the metaphor of the vine and the branches. His description consists of only seventeen verses, and this word picture of abiding in Jesus is found only in the Gospel of John. Jesus gave it at the very end of his ministry, just before he went to the cross.

Although this passage is relatively short, numerous people have credited Jesus' brief teaching revolving around the simple words, "Abide in me," as the source of the joy in their lives and the power to impact the lives of others. So don't think less of these seventeen verses because of their brevity or simplicity. It's exciting that so much treasure is found in such a small package! It takes only a minute or two to open, but it takes a lifetime to unpack.

We will divide Jesus' lesson on abiding into two parts. In this chapter, we'll look at verses 1–8, where he describes the metaphor of the vine and branches. In chapter 9, we'll delve into verses 9–17 where he explains the abiding friendship.

If you live most of each day in a close, abiding relationship with Jesus, you know the serenity of having the King of kings, who calls you friend, walking by your side through the uncertainty and challenges of each day. You know the excitement of being an instrument God uses to impact the lives of others in significant ways.

Let's explore Jesus' intimate words to his disciples and us and learn how we can have a deeper friendship with him.

Roles—Verses 1 and 5

The first few verses of John 15 record how Jesus laid out the roles involved in our abiding relationship with him. Notice four key words continue to show up throughout the passage: "abide," "vine," "branches," and "fruit."

> "I am the **true vine,** and my Father is the vinedresser." (John 15:1)

> "I am **the vine;** you are the branches. Whoever abides in me and I in him, he it is that bears much fruit, for apart from me you can do nothing." (John 15:5)

In verse 1, Jesus tells us he is the vine, God the Father is the gardener or the vinedresser, and we are the branches.

The Father is the caretaker. He cares for those whom he has chosen—you and me. Jesus is the vine. He is the source of life. His life is flowing into us. We are the branches. The branch itself has no life. The vine has the life, and when the branch is attached to the vine, the life of the vine flows into and through the branch, and grapes are produced from the connection.

Note that Jesus did not choose a large tree with strong branches that can grow tall and impressive, independent of a caretaker. To describe our relationship with him, he chose a vine whose branches are scrawny and feeble. The branches of a vine need a great deal of care to reach their peak fruitfulness. When cared for properly, a vineyard can be both beautiful and productive.

On our tenth wedding anniversary, Juli and I traveled to Napa Valley, California. If you've ever been there, you know it's a valley filled with large, lovely vineyards. While a lot of fruit bearing is occurring, there's very little noise. In effect, Napa Valley is a production facility for wine. But one distinction that makes this wine region stand out from so many other production facilities in the world is that the vineyards are peaceful, calm, and restful.

In the midst of the peaceful environment, under the watchful eyes of their caretakers, the vines are going about their moment-by-moment purpose of flowing their life into the branches and producing a staggering amount of some of the best grapes in the world. As the vinedressers go about their work, no grunting and groaning is going on among the vines and branches. They are quietly and peacefully bearing much fruit.

While Jesus names the Father, the Son, and us (the branches), he doesn't specifically name the Holy Spirit. But just as the hidden, life-giving sap flows from the vine into the branches, so does the Holy Spirit flow into us as we remain connected to (abide in) Jesus, the vine. The result in both the vineyard and our spiritual lives is bearing fruit.

As the fruit in the vineyard bears witness to the connection of the vine to the branch, so does the fruit in our lives bear witness to Jesus' life flowing into us in the person of the Holy Spirit. The fruit of the vine is the evidence that the life of the vine is flowing through the branch. As you abide in Jesus and receive the flow of the Spirit into your life, the fruit you bear gives evidence to the life of Jesus in you.

Relationship—Verses 4 and 5

> "Abide in me, and I in you. As the branch cannot bear fruit by itself, unless it abides in the vine, neither can you, unless you abide in me. I am the vine; you are the branches. Whoever abides in me and I in him, he it is that bears much fruit, for apart from me you can do nothing." (John 15:4–5)

Another word for abide is "remain." In this context, abide means to remain in constant relationship with Jesus. Abiding describes an ongoing, intimate fellowship with Jesus. As the branches, we are to remain in continuous fellowship with our friend, Savior, and source of life—Jesus the vine.

It's interesting to note the word "nothing" at the end of verse 5. In many Bible passages, it is not uncommon for English-language versions of the Bible to translate or interpret words differently. But when you look at John 15:5 in some of the more commonly used versions of the Bible, here's what you find:

> New American Standard version: "apart from me, you can do **nothing**."
> New International Version: "apart from me, you can do **nothing**."
> English Standard Version: "apart from me, you can do **nothing**."
> New King James Version: "for without Me you can do **nothing**."

Different scholars looked at the meaning of this verse, and in each case chose the word "nothing" to describe what Jesus said we could do on our own. In other words, there's consensus among these scholars that "nothing" is how Jesus described what we can accomplish without him.

As we are about to see, however, even our non-abiding moments can be fruitful. Jesus is making it clear: even when we are not fully engaged with him, the fruit we see in our lives is still a result of his life flowing through us, not a result of our own fleshly efforts.

Level II—Modest Fruit Bearing

> "Every branch in me that does **not bear fruit** he takes away, and every branch that **does bear fruit** he prunes, that it may bear **more fruit**." (John 15:2)

Our lives display different degrees of fruit bearing, based on our relationship with Jesus. In John 15:2, Jesus describes the fruit we bear when we are abiding in him in three ways: no fruit, fruit, and more fruit. We are not completely useless to God if we are operating in the flesh. He is able to work through anyone at any time if he chooses. It is still possible to be used by God when we are operating in our no-good flesh and living in Level II.

There's no need to become discouraged when your obedience is less than perfect. Thankfully, by his grace, God can use us even when we are not abiding in Jesus! However, God's plan for you is greater than these modest results described in verse 2. God's plan is for your abiding life to bear *much fruit!*

Level III—Abundant Fruit Bearing

> "I am the vine; you are the branches. Whoever abides in me and I in him, he it is that **bears much fruit**, for apart from me you can do nothing." (John 15:5)

In verse 5, Jesus lays out a new level of fruit bearing. He says, "Whoever abides in me and I in him … bears much fruit." Previously, in verse 2, which describes non-abiding living, Jesus described the lesser fruit bearing as either no fruit, fruit, or more fruit. Now, in this new way of living, as you are abiding in Jesus, he says you will become a bearer of *much* fruit.

As you abide in Jesus, your fruitfulness increases dramatically. You bring greater glory to God by the impact your life has on your world. A different level of relationship results in a greater magnitude of fruit bearing.

When you abide in Jesus, you *will* bear much fruit. You cannot abide in Jesus and not bear *much* fruit. This is another of one of Jesus' exciting conditional promises. He didn't say, "If you abide in me, you *might* bear fruit." He said, "You *will* bear *much* fruit."

When describing abiding in him, Jesus explains that this is a new and more fruitful way of living, and it's only experienced by staying connected to him. Only by having intimate fellowship with Jesus do you experience the fullness of him living his life in and through yours. Abiding means intimate fellowship with Jesus. When you're abiding, you're dwelling in a rich relationship with Jesus.

The Great 2 for 1

In the previous chapter, we said The Great 2 for 1 means that as you abide in Jesus, you're being filled with the Holy Spirit. We can now see the evidence of the abiding, Spirit-filled life is seen in its fruit. The sign you are filled with the Spirit is *internal fruit*—love, joy, peace, patience, kindness, goodness faithfulness, gentleness, and self-control. The sign you are abiding in Jesus is the *external fruit*—bearing *much fruit*. As you abide, you experience both the internal fruit of the Spirit and the external impact through your life. To summarize: one obedience (abide), two blessings (internal and external fruit). The Great 2 for 1!

As you abide in Jesus, you also get to know him better. And since abiding in Jesus fills you with the Holy Spirit, abiding results in you getting to know the person of the Holy Spirit better as well. Staying connected to Jesus moment-by-moment throughout the day will better acquaint you with the ways of both Jesus and the Holy Spirit.

Experiencing the Desires of Your Heart

> Delight yourself in the LORD, and he will give you **the desires of your heart.** (Psalm 37:4)

When we abide, we are in the Abiding Room. We experience all the blessings of Level III living. This is the abundant life Jesus promised. The answer to the desires of our hearts is to abide in Jesus.

Jesus tells us another blessing of abiding in him is answered prayer.

> **"If you abide in me,** and my words abide in you, ask whatever you wish, and it will be done for you." (John 15:7)

Long before God revealed to me how to walk in the Spirit, Juli was living it. In the midst of my harsh, critical behavior, she was filled with gentleness, patience, and kindness. Though I saw her living it daily and heard it taught in our church, I wouldn't listen. Juli had tried everything to get through to me, and we had been to marriage counselors on multiple occasions. But despite the fact that I refused to change, Juli trusted God and kept praying.

I needed a jolt to my attitude, and God heard Juli's prayers and gave me that jolt when I saw my young son in hysterics after my dish-smashing incident. God did a miracle in my heart and our marriage.

Jesus said, "For truly, I say to you, if you have faith like a grain of mustard seed, you will say to this **mountain, 'Move** from here to there,' and it will **move,** and nothing will be impossible for you" (Matthew 17:20).

While there is no guarantee that it will play out in everyone's life exactly as it did in ours, Juli and I can testify that the promise of a mountain being moved was true in our marriage. Juli is a faithful abider. She persisted in prayer and God moved our mountain—my harsh and critical spirit—and we give him praise.

What is the desire of your heart to see God do? Jesus says first to abide in him, and then to pray.

Your Purpose on Earth

> "By this my Father is glorified, that you bear much fruit and so prove to be my disciples." (John 15:8)

Did you notice when you got saved, you didn't immediately get promoted to heaven? Why is that? If God is love and wants the best for you, why didn't you go directly to heaven when you were first saved? As a loving Father, why didn't he remove you from this troubled, fallen world?

The reason is he still has work for you to do! Work that will bring him glory. In his sovereign wisdom, God has chosen to use ordinary people like us to glorify himself as we live out our lives here on earth. The glory isn't for us, it's for God. When Jesus uses the phrase "bear fruit," he is saying he wants our lives to bless others wherever he places us.

Whatever kind of work he might have you doing right now is intended to bless others for his glory. When people see you living the abiding, Spirit-filled life, God will draw others to you and to Jesus because of what you are doing by his power.

Like the actual physical vineyards, the spiritual work of the branches is done by the vinedresser and the vine. The branches are effortlessly filled with the life of the vine, and the harvest of fruit appears as the result for all to see. Observers look at the feeble branches and know they couldn't have possibly done it on their own, so it must have been the work of the vinedresser and the vine. When others are impacted, they don't admire the scrawny branch; they admire the Vinedresser—God.

The apostle Paul described it this way: "For we are his workmanship, created in Christ Jesus for good works, which God prepared beforehand, that we should walk in them" (Ephesians 2:10). God saved you for a *relationship* with him, but he kept you on earth for *good works*.

Your one-on-one relationship with Jesus is not just so you can have joy and peace *internally* but so you'll have a great impact *externally* as well. The abiding branch is connected to Jesus on one end, but bearing much fruit on the other—fruit that is for the benefit of others.

Fruit bearing is not meant to be a solo act. The vine has many branches. Two thousand years ago, when Jesus said "you," he wasn't just talking to the apostle John, whose writing we read in John 15. He meant "you" as in "all you guys"—all eleven disciples who were in the room. And when we read it today, it is still plural. Jesus is speaking to all of us collectively in the church. Jesus, the vine, intends for us all, as his branches, to be big-time fruit bearers together in our own vineyards—the local church.

Imagine the dynamic impact of a local church filled with people abiding in Jesus and continuously filled with the Holy Spirit. This is what turned the world upside down 2,000 years ago, and it can turn the world upside down again!

When you abide in Jesus and are filled with the Holy Spirit, God will use your life in exciting and substantial ways you could never have imagined. You'll gain a greater understanding that the way God made you divinely fits into the way he uses you. Perhaps for the first time, you will have confidence in knowing why you exist!

ABIDING TRUTH

When you abide in Jesus,
you will bear much fruit.

REFLECTION QUESTIONS

1. The essence of the vine and the branches is about our dependence on Jesus. How does depending on him make you feel? What might it look like to be more dependent on him than you are now?

2. What are the key differences between someone who is not bearing fruit, someone who is bearing some fruit, and someone who is bearing much fruit?

3. When you consider the idea of abiding in Jesus, what does that look like? (Think about others you know who have a great relationship with Jesus. What are they doing?)

4. Which one or two fruit of the Spirit do you wish you were bearing more of? How can spending more time with Jesus make that desire a reality?

SONG SUGGESTIONS

"New Wine" by Hillsong Worship
"Abide With Me" by The Worship Initiative, featuring Bethany Barnard and John Marc Kohl
"Tend" by Bethel Music, and Emmy Rose

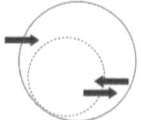

CHAPTER 9

The Abiding Friendship

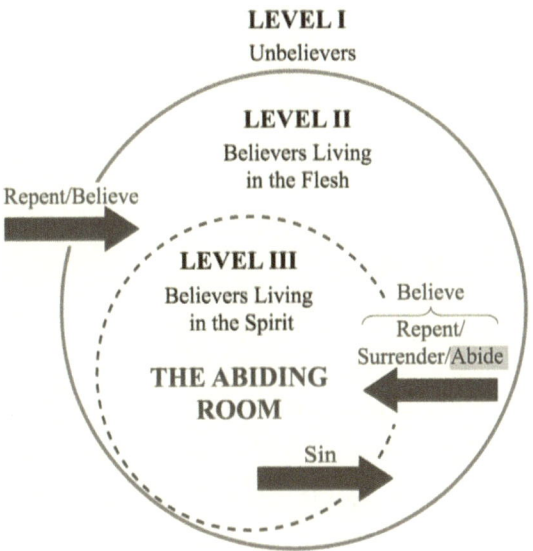

"As the Father has loved me, so have I loved you. Abide in my love. If you keep my commandments, you will abide in my love, just as I have kept my Father's commandments and abide in his love. These things I have spoken to you, that my joy may be in you, and that your joy may be full. This is my commandment, that you love one another as I have loved you. Greater love has no one than this, that someone lay down his life for his friends. You are my friends if you do what I command you. No longer do I call you servants, for the servant does not know what his master is doing; but I have called you friends, for all that I have heard from my Father I have made known to you. You did not choose me, but I chose you and appointed you that you should go and bear fruit and that your fruit should abide, so that whatever you ask the Father in my name, he may give it to you. These things I command you, so that you will love one another." (John 15:9–17)

In chapter 8, we studied the first eight verses of John 15 in which Jesus illustrated that the bearing of much fruit is fulfilled by our abiding relationship with him. Now in verses 9–17, he describes this relationship in very personal and relational terms. In these verses, Jesus applies the vine and branch metaphor to his abiding friendship with his disciples, which includes us.

Hopefully the term "friendship" describes your existing relationship with Jesus. But regardless of how you may currently describe your relationship with Jesus, in this chapter we'll learn how you can deepen that relationship.

Your Friendship with Jesus

In John 15:15, Jesus describes to his disciples (and us) what the abiding friendship looks like: "No longer do I call you servants, for the servant does not know what his master is doing; but I have called you **friends**, for all that I have heard from my Father I have made known to you."

When you think of the people you call your close friends, what comes to mind? What do you do with a good friend? You spend time with them. You enjoy each other's company. You laugh. You tell each other your hopes, dreams, and fears. You enjoy and trust them.

Well, that's exactly how Jesus thinks of you—*as his friend!* Jesus doesn't just love you—*he likes you!* That's why these are the same things Jesus wants to do with you on a daily basis. He not only loves you enough to save you, he enjoys you and longs to be with you every minute of every day.

The Joy of Abiding

On his last night before the cross, after telling his disciples about abiding for the first time, Jesus said, "I have told you this so that my joy may be in you and that your joy may be complete" (John 15:11 NIV). He was telling them they would be joyful regardless of their circumstances if they remained in relationship with him.

The same is true for you today. The good news is Jesus has given you the key to your own joy! Even in times of turmoil—health problems, financial issues, a job loss, others' antagonism toward your faith—we can still have joy. Joy is spiritual because it comes from God. God and his Holy Spirit never change, so you can be joyful regardless of your situation. Unlike happiness, which is dependent on the unpredictable circumstances of the world, joy is available at any time to you when you're abiding in Jesus.

What Does Abiding Look Like in Your Life?

Christ in you, the hope of glory. (Colossians 1:27 NIV)

What is abiding? Earlier, I talked about how calm, quiet, and peaceful the vineyards of Napa Valley are. Abiding is a restful, obedient activity. It's not lazy or inactive. It is peace in the midst of obediently carrying out your work. Abiding in Jesus is letting Christ live out his life in and through you by the power of the Holy Spirit.

Abiding means you're in tune with the amazing reality that Jesus is right beside you. Regardless of the circumstances, you are with Jesus. He's always with you in all things. He's right here, right now. Having Jesus alongside you in an abiding relationship makes any of life's experiences better.

Abiding means staying in harmony, in fellowship, and in union with Jesus. As you walk through your day with him, the truths you read in the Bible about him are no longer just words on a page; they come alive through your life. For instance, the patience of Jesus you read about becomes reality in your life as Jesus lives out his patience through you. The peace of Jesus is lived out in your heart and mind, even in the surprises and setbacks of the day. Just as Jesus was never truly alone because he and the Father were one, you, too, are never alone because you are one with him.

It's often easy to turn our faith into an expectation of performance. But practicing the presence of Jesus as we go through our day turns what can become religion into a loving relationship with him. It's not a checklist to constrain you or a restrictive set of rules to follow, but rather a restful relationship that actually frees you from slavery to them.

You can confidently rest on Jesus' promises in each area of your life as you acknowledge and understand he is always available to you, and you make yourself available to him. When you mess up or drift away from him, don't ignore it or agonize over it. Quickly acknowledge it (that is called confession), ask him for help, then simply and confidently move on.

Acknowledging our mistakes with Jesus is much easier than addressing our mistakes with other people. Since we often have trouble getting over our mistakes, we incorrectly assume it's the same with him. But Jesus is loving, caring, kind, and gentle. He loves you and is eager to forgive, instruct, reconnect, and move forward with you.

Be reassured by this promise God made to Israel, which is also a promise to us: "For I will be merciful toward their iniquities, and I will remember their sins no more" (Hebrews 8:12). Should you stumble, Jesus' grace, mercy, love, kindness, and gentleness that you experienced when you first began a relationship with him is always available to you. Go to him quickly and be refreshed. Jesus loves you.

And let's say it again—*Jesus likes you!* He calls you *friend!* There is nothing he wants more than to hang out with you. That's why he made you his—to walk alongside you all day, every day. He wants to talk about what you are going through today and guide you through it.

Over the years, when Juli has seen my driven nature take over and found me having trouble slowing down and relaxing, she's often reminded me, "Resting *is* accomplishing something." Perhaps we can borrow from Juli's wisdom, apply it to the counterintuitive nature of abiding, and say, "Simply abiding *is* accomplishing something."

I'm still learning to not approach Jesus just to receive something from him. Instead, we are to go to Jesus to just enjoy Jesus. Just resting in Jesus. Just Jesus. Take heart in knowing there is nothing better than simply resting in him. Nothing we accomplish in our feeble strength compares to simply enjoying staying connected to him.

God wants us to become receivers, not achievers. The trying and the striving in our limited strength, even if the intentions are good, is not God's way. He wants us to be fruit bearers, not fruit producers or achievers. Jesus didn't say, "I want you to go out and *produce* fruit." He said, *"Bear* much fruit."

As we discussed in the previous chapter, bearing much fruit is a certainty as we abide in Jesus. Remaining connected to him is the first and foremost thing. Abiding not only takes priority ahead of even doing the ministry God has called us to, but is actually how Jesus intends for ministry itself to be done. By our staying joined to him, Jesus actually does the ministry in and through us, rather than our attempting to do it through our own self-effort.

Obedience Maintains the Abiding Connection

Once begun, how do you keep abiding? Jesus explained it to his disciples this way: "If you **keep my commandments,** you will abide in my **love,** just as I have **kept my Father's commandments** and abide in his **love**" (John 15:10). And earlier in the evening he had said similarly, "If you **love** me, you will **keep my commandments**" (John 14:15).

In these verses, Jesus says the way you *continue* to abide is by obeying what God instructs you to do through his Word and his Spirit. These words are firm instruction regarding your friendship with Jesus, describing how to *maintain* the special, intimate, abiding friendship with him. Jesus is explaining that you can continue enjoying the fullness of your moment-by-moment abiding relationship with him through moment-by-moment obedience.

How do you know if you are abiding in Jesus? Since abiding in Jesus causes you to be filled with the Holy Spirit, the confirmation that you are abiding is the *same* as the confirmation that you are filled with the Spirit—do a fruit inspection. If you sense the fruit of the Spirit at work in you—love, joy, peace, patience, kindness, goodness, faithfulness, gentleness, and self-control—then you know you are abiding in Jesus. At any moment, a fruit inspection can reveal whether you are *a part of* the vine, or *apart from* the vine.

But regardless of where you are at any given moment, remember Jesus is always waiting and available to regain full connection and fellowship with you. He loves you, enjoys being with you, and is always lovingly waiting to be asked to guide you.

"Here I am! I stand at the door and knock. If anyone hears my voice and opens the door, I will come in and eat with that person, and they with me." (Revelation 3:20 NIV)

A Biblical Example: Mary the Abider of Bethany

The Bible has an encouraging story for all of us ordinary people. Some people might say, "Well, you know, I've never had lots of blessings, I'm not sure I'm that kind of person." Let's look at someone in the Bible who was an *ordinary, common person* who had a *wonderful, intimate friendship* with Jesus and was commended by him for it. Her name was Mary of Bethany. I like to call her, Mary the Abider of Bethany.

Mary of Bethany was the sister of Lazarus and Martha, and perhaps as much as anyone in the Bible, Mary understood what it meant to abide in Jesus. Luke 10:38–42 tells the story:

> As Jesus and his disciples were on their way, he came to a village where a woman named Martha opened her home to him. She had a sister called Mary, who sat at the Lord's feet listening to what he said. But Martha was distracted by all the preparations that had to be made. She came to him and asked, "Lord, don't you care that my sister has left me to do the work by myself? Tell her to help me!"
>
> "Martha, Martha" the Lord answered, "You are worried and upset about many things. But few things are needed—**or indeed only one.** Mary has **chosen** what is better and **it will not be taken away from her.**" (NIV)

In the last part of his response to Martha, Jesus makes three statements that contain significant truths for us to embrace today:

1. *Only one thing is needed.* Though there was much to do, Mary did only one thing—stay near Jesus and listen to him.
2. *Doing the one thing is a choice.* Mary made a choice—to remain and rest in Jesus' presence. She chose to be with him over all the other things she could have chosen.

3. *It will not be taken away*. Mary's experience of being close to Jesus and learning from him would always be available to her. Similarly, its impact on her would be permanent. The same is true for you today. That's so reassuring, isn't it? In a world where friends, family, finances, health, etc., can be taken away, this one thing (the better thing) cannot be taken away—your abiding relationship with Jesus.

Jesus' Comforting Presence During Difficulties

Though the abiding, Spirit-filled life comes with the promise of the love, joy, and peace of Jesus, and the bearing of much fruit, it does *not* come with the promise of a life without difficulty. Jesus' promise and provision is that he will be right next to you as you go through hardship. As others have said, Jesus doesn't keep you from the fire; he's with you in the fire. Jesus doesn't keep you from the valley; he's with you in the valley. Your problems aren't extinguished, but they stay in proper perspective.

In fact, God may allow hardships in your life in order to put your faith in him on display to others. What is better evidence of Jesus' life being lived in and through you than when you handle trials and difficulties with joy and peace?

When you are filled with the Holy Spirit despite hardships, others—even those who may have never set foot in a church—may begin to ask themselves or ask you directly how you're able to cope with these challenges. They may begin to wonder how you're able to approach each day with such calmness when others are anxious or angry. Often, that's the beginning of God using your abiding life to bear much fruit!

When you're living the abiding, Spirit-filled life, your life will impact those around you as they see you living above your circumstances. Your spouse, family, friends, co-workers, and neighbors cannot help being attracted to your joy and peace in the midst of life's uncertainties. Godly character itself bears fruit that remains.

Here are some encouraging words from the Bible reminding us that God is with us during trials:

*God will **guide** you in the midst of your trial:*

> Whether you turn to the right or to the left, your ears will hear a voice behind you, saying, "This is the way; walk in it." (Isaiah 30:21 NIV)

> "I will lead the blind by ways they have not known, along unfamiliar paths I will guide them; I will turn the darkness into light before them and make the rough places smooth. These are the things I will do; I will not forsake them." (Isaiah 42:16 NIV)

*God will **comfort** you in the midst of your trial:*

> The LORD is good, a refuge in times of trouble. He cares for those who trust in him. (Nahum 1:7 NIV)

> Cast your cares on the LORD and he will sustain you; he will never let the righteous be shaken. (Psalm 55:22 NIV)

*God will **help** you in the midst of your trial:*

> Though he may stumble, he will not fall, for the LORD upholds him with his hand. (Psalm 37:24 NIV)

> The LORD is a refuge for the oppressed, a strong hold in times of trouble. (Psalm 9:9 NIV)

> God is our refuge and strength, an ever-present help in trouble. Therefore we will not fear, though the earth give way and the mountains fall into the heart of the sea, though its waters roar and foam and the mountains quake with their surging. (Psalm 46:1–3 NIV)

*God will **restore** you after the trial:*

> And after you have suffered a little while, the God of all grace, who has called you to his eternal glory in Christ, will himself restore, confirm, strengthen, and establish you. (1 Peter 5:10)

Journaling

Consider journaling. Journaling will allow you to capture what is going on in your life and what God seems to be saying to you, and will connect the two. Use any type of journal. It doesn't need to be fancy. I use inexpensive spiral-bound notebooks. Keep your journal beside you when you do any type of Bible study. If something is impressed on your heart, jot it down. You could even start by using one of the verses listed above and thank God for how he was with you in the midst of a trial.

Don't be concerned about the quality of your writing. Just get it on paper. Write the private thoughts of your heart to Jesus, not to others. Every few days, go back and see what's been happening and ask God to reveal to you what he's showing you from the events and thoughts of your life.

I dislike writing but am very glad I have kept a journal for many years. My journals are pretty much a scribbly mess, and much of it shows my confusion, frustration, and so on. There is no attempt to be profound. Some days nothing is written, some days a little is written, and some days a lot is written. Each time I write, I start a new page, even if the previous entry was very short. There's no particular pattern, other than many start with *Lord, you are showing me ...* or *Lord, thank you for ...* But strung together, they show the blessings of God's leading in my life.

You can journal in any style that fits you. The important point is you're in consistent communication with God and are creating a record of his work in your life. As you look back, you can thank him and praise him for his loving provision.

Abide in Jesus and Be Filled with the Holy Spirit

Jesus instructs you to abide in him and promises he will abide in you. Rest in him, and he will rest in you. He's always there for you. He's always waiting for you. He won't turn you down. But it's your choice. Abiding in Jesus is choosing Level III living in the Abiding Room.

Spend a few minutes in prayer, resting in Jesus' presence and sensing what the Holy Spirit is saying to you.

ABIDING TRUTH

Jesus calls you friend
and enjoys spending time with you.

REFLECTION QUESTIONS

1. When you think of the word "friend," what or who springs to mind? What are a few traits that make someone a good friend?

2. In John 15:13, Jesus says "Greater love has no one than this, that someone lay down his life for his friends." What does this mean to you and your relationship with him?

3. One of the keys to an effective friendship (or any relationship) is spending time with the other person. What are some of your favorite ways to spend time with Jesus? Why is it important for Jesus-followers to spend time with him?

4. Take a few moments to examine your relationship with Jesus. What's good? What's missing? What feels confusing? What needs to change?

5. As you start each day in the coming week, ask yourself, *"What is one blessing of being friends with Jesus?"* Write each one down in your journal and review it each morning before adding to this list.

SONG SUGGESTIONS

"I Am" by Jill Phillips
"Christ In Me" by Jeremy Camp
"Just Give Me Jesus" by Unspoken

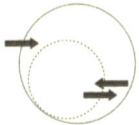

Part Four

SURRENDER

CHAPTER 10

Surrender Your Will

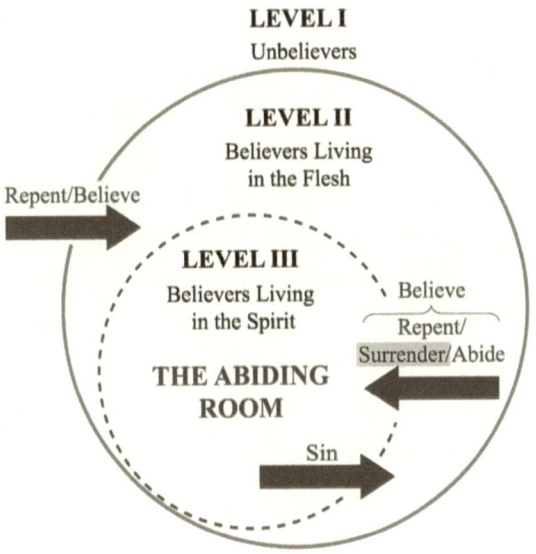

"Not my will, but yours, be done." (Luke 22:42)

As we begin the chapters on Surrender, the word "Surrender" is shaded in the diagram.

We now know the key to being filled with the Holy Spirit is abiding in Jesus. This means the reason so few Christians are consistently experiencing the abiding, Spirit-filled life is because they aren't abiding in Jesus. Why is that? I believe the primary reason is simply very few are aware abiding exists and what it entails. Hopefully, the information presented on these pages will help enlighten and inspire many in that regard.

First, it's important to explore what prevents us from abiding. I think two primary barriers exist for most of us: (1) living for ourselves in the flesh, and (2) sin. Before we can truly abide in Jesus, we must address the effect the flesh and sin have on our lives. The remedy for living in the flesh is surrender, which we will explore in the next three chapters. After that, we'll consider the remedy for sin, which is repentance.

Before we proceed, let's briefly look at the words we'll be using. While most things in our spiritual lives exist in varying degrees, in the next few chapters we'll use absolute and direct terms to make the point about the importance of the abiding, Spirit-filled life. The assumption is that experiencing the full, consistent blessings of the abiding, Spirit-filled life explained in the *preceding* chapters is only possible if we are obedient to the instruction on surrender and repentance in the *upcoming* chapters.

In some cases, we'll be speaking as if the area being addressed is either all or nothing. We will say things along the lines of, "If you want to receive the full benefits, you must pay the full cost." The hope is that, in our making direct and absolute statements, you will experience an increase in the quality of your life and, ultimately, greater eternal rewards.

Therefore, keep in mind we are using emphatic words for only one purpose: to experience more of the abiding, Spirit-filled life now, and in anticipation of the day when Jesus says to you, "Well done, good and faithful servant" (see Matthew 25:23).

In addition, it's worth noting we'll use the term "surrender" to refer to the surrender of our will to God's will *after* our salvation. Surrender is the ongoing, repeated, daily act of surrendering our will to the Father's will. Surrender may be known by other names, such as abandon, release, relinquish, or yield. All these terms imply the giving up of ourselves and our rights to Jesus and trusting in his indwelling Holy Spirit to bring about the desires of our hearts in his time and his way.

What might the absolute surrender of your whole heart look like? Let's explore the possibilities.

The Ultimate Surrendered Life

The ultimate example of a surrendered life, of course, is Jesus. Perhaps as amazing as the fact that Jesus *lived* a perfect life, is that he *left* a perfect life. He surrendered his rights and left his perfect life in heaven to be nailed to a cross for us on earth. He did not consider himself first. In fact, he did not consider himself at all.

The Bible describes Jesus' surrender to God the Father this way:

> Do nothing from selfish ambition or conceit, but in humility count others more significant than yourselves. Let each of you look not only to his own interests, but also to the interests of others. Have this mind among yourselves, which is yours in Christ Jesus, who, though he was in the form of God, did not count equality with God a thing to be grasped, but **emptied himself,** by taking the **form of a servant,** being born in the **likeness of men**. And being found in human form, **he humbled himself by becoming obedient** to the point of death, even death on a cross. Therefore God has highly exalted him and bestowed on him the name that is above every name, so that at the name of Jesus every knee should bow, in heaven and on earth and under the earth, and every tongue confess that Jesus Christ is Lord, to the glory of God the Father. (Philippians 2:3–11)

As we humble ourselves and surrender our will to the Father's will as Jesus did, our hearts come into alignment with his plans for our lives. Then we can fully know the joy of living out the purpose for which God created us.

Remember, God wants you to experience him in fullness even in the seemingly minor moments of the day. These minor moments are the pathway to the major plan he laid out for you since the time he chose to create you!

> For we are his workmanship, created in Christ Jesus for good works, which God prepared beforehand, that we should walk in them. (Ephesians 2:10)

God's Way or Your Way?

Too often my plans, strategies, and tactics take me off course and bear little fruit. This occurs because of my independence from God rather than the perfect will of God playing out as a result of my surrender and dependence on Jesus.

In many ways, our ongoing spiritual battle is the opposite of a physical battle. In physical battles, you throw all your effort into pummeling the enemy into submission until they surrender and the battle ends. In contrast, to win the spiritual struggle between our flesh and the Spirit, we must *begin* with surrender. Victory in the spiritual battle within us is assured when we surrender at the outset.

As you follow the example of surrender Jesus modeled, and surrender your rights to self, you can trust the indwelling Holy Spirit to do the work in and through you. Giving up your independent ways sets you on the path leading to victory over your flesh.

Surrender Your Comfort

The fullest blessings of God follow the person living in wholehearted surrender. God sees our hearts as surrendered when they are emptied of our self-centered plans and in a state of ready obedience to his will. Surrender often means leaving the comfortable present circumstances we know for the unknown future God has planned for us.

Let's look at two biblical examples of people whose surrender meant leaving the life they knew to follow God wherever he led them. The first example is Abraham in the Old Testament, and the second is Peter and the disciples in the New Testament.

The earthly blessing Abraham and the disciples received was the result of abandoning their agendas and accepting God's invitation to follow his plan for their lives. While we don't know exactly what they gave up, we do know they couldn't have experienced the blessings God had in store for them if they had clung tightly to the safety of their present circumstances. These principles of the blessing of surrender are still true in your life today.

We might not even know Abraham's name (which was Abram at the time of God's invitation) if he hadn't left behind the life he knew for the unknown life God invited him into. Because Abraham trusted God, he became the father of the Jewish nation:

> The LORD had said to Abram, "**Go** from your country, your people and your father's household to the land I will show you. I will make you into a great nation, and **I will bless you;** I will make your name great, and **you will be a blessing.**" (Genesis 12:1–2 NIV)

> By faith Abraham obeyed when he was called to go out to a place that he was to receive as an inheritance. And he went out, **not knowing where he was going.** (Hebrews 11:8)

It's also unlikely we would know the disciples' names if they hadn't left behind the lives they knew for the unknown plans God had for them. In a dialogue found in the Gospels of Matthew, Mark, and Luke, the apostle Peter expressed the disciples' surrender to Jesus in this way:

> And Peter said, "See, we have left our homes and followed you." (Luke 18:28)

Jesus responded to Peter with this affirmation of their surrender and the blessings that follow it:

> And he said to them, "Truly, I say to you, there is no one who has left house or wife or brothers or parents or children, for the sake of the kingdom of God, who will not receive many times more in this time, and in the age to come eternal life." (Luke 18:29–30)

Acknowledge God Is in Control

Years ago, a Christian woman working in our office told me she'd observed God's blessing on our financial planning practice in ways I hadn't realized. When I took the time to look, I saw she was right. God was doing a far better job of marketing the business than I was.

Going against all my tendencies to devise my own plans, I decided to surrender control of my attempts to grow our small business and made God our "Director of Marketing." Though I had not yet reached my goals for where I hoped the business would grow, I made some moves to trust God to take it wherever he wanted it to go.

Those were the days when the internet was in its infancy and had not yet become the means of promotion it is today. Yellow Pages advertising had proven a very reliable means of obtaining new clients with no effort at a reasonable cost. But the Holy Spirit seemed to be telling me that, as a step of faith, I should discontinue Yellow Pages advertising and rely solely on God. I canceled all of our ads and trusted God to continue to bring in new clients however he wished.

Not only did God bless this trust and surrender of my strategies by bringing in additional high-quality clients, but without any effort on my part, he blessed us further by providing new staff with unique skills and qualities on whom I could place greater reliance. I was able to focus more of my attention on our clients' and staff's needs and felt a great burden lifted off my shoulders.

It sounds a little silly, but because God did such a great job as Director of Marketing, I did something I should have done at the beginning: I surrendered all aspects of the business to him. I acknowledged what had been true all along—God owned the business, and I was his worker. As I yielded to God's direction, I became more relaxed, and the work became more enjoyable for both my staff and me.

For the first time, my work took on the form of "tentmaking," which is a term the Bible uses to describe how the apostle Paul provided for his financial needs (Acts 18:3). He made tents. Instead of focusing so intently on my role as a small business owner, my attention was freed up for the kingdom work God had planned for me outside of the office.

Surrender Daily

What might surrender look like in your life? Is it possible Jesus is the Lord of your life but not the Lord of your today? Is it possible you turn to him for the big, insurmountable obstacles that occur occasionally in your life but don't give him all the little things that are occurring every moment of the day?

Surrender can look as simple as beginning each day with heartfelt attitudes and prayers, such as:

Lord, this day is yours. I'm going to trust you for everything today.
Lord, not my will, but your will be done today.
Lord, I have no idea what this day looks like, but you do, so I'm giving it to you and trusting you for it.
Lord, I surrender control of this day to you. Take it and use me for your glory.
Lord, show me how to be your hands and feet today.

An attitude of surrender sets your heart and mind on trusting God to guide you through the upcoming day. A surrendered heart keeps your chocolate milk stirred up. What a wonderful blessing it is to live with a heart fully surrendered to and trusting in Jesus!

Fasting from Self

When we're in the flesh, we're very likely motivated by our desire to be esteemed, noticed, admired, and respected by others. Sometimes we long to be the center of attention. With the immense influence of social media today, many sources encourage us to put the focus on ourselves in an attempt to portray ourselves in a positive light. This can become habitual.

As you may know, when the Bible speaks of fasting, it means going without something for a period of time in order to focus on God, to pray about something in particular, and to listen to and hear from God. As I've discipled young men, an exercise I've found enlightening is what I call "Fasting from Self." For three days, the young men try to fast from self by doing as little as possible to draw attention to themselves in both writing and conversation. I encourage you to try this too.

Here's what it involves:

- Don't tell anyone you're taking the challenge.
- For three days—if possible, including the weekend when you're more likely to be around friends and family—don't talk about yourself.

- Participate in conversations, but don't express your own opinions.
- If the conversation turns to you, respond briefly, and, without being too obvious, turn it back to others.
- If someone expresses an opinion that's the opposite of yours, hold back from expressing yours.
- Humble yourself and be genuinely interested in anyone and any topic. Don't redirect the conversation to something that interests you, even if you are bored and you completely disagree with what's being discussed.
- If you find yourself in a discussion that seems to have no end in sight, or participating in something that is completely disinteresting to you, stay engaged and enjoy it.
- Last, take a break from posting anything on social media.

Based on my experience personally and on the experiences of others who have tried this, you may be very surprised at what occurs. Many people stumble at the outset and simply quit. One young man's experience was quite humorous. He was with his adult siblings at a family weekend event and didn't get past the first hour before his siblings noticed the difference in him, pointedly asking, "What are you doing?" When he focused his interactions on others, it was noticeable to those who knew him best!

If you feel led to try this, you may be surprised at how many times you want to express an opinion or draw attention to yourself. It can be a challenge to yield yourself to such a seemingly easy task, but it may reveal something that will bless your obedience in practicing surrender.

Surrender to God's Plan for You

> "For I know the plans I have for you," declares the LORD, "plans to prosper you and not to harm you, plans to give you hope and a future." (Jeremiah 29:11 NIV)

Although this beloved message from God is directed to the Israelites as a people group, Jeremiah 29:11 describes God's heart for all his children. God has a unique plan for you too. And if you look in the rearview mirror of your life, you can probably see how God has blessed you when you listened to his directions in the past. You celebrate when you think about these times of trusting him.

But you may also remember choices you've made to go your own way that brought regret. Everyone can look back and see both types of experiences. Take a moment to recall some choices in your past, both good and bad.

You undoubtedly also remember times when the Holy Spirit gave you whispers, hints, and nudges, telling you which way to go. Sometimes you chose to listen to them, and sometimes you chose to ignore them. These experiences remind you of the value of listening to the Spirit's guidance.

When you completely yield your life to God and abide in Jesus, you can hear the Holy Spirit more clearly as he guides you in the next direction you should go. The view out the front window is not always clear. That's the point. You have to trust God for where he is taking you and listen to instructions for the next turn. As a follower of Jesus, when you come to a decision point in your life, you can have confidence that the Holy Spirit living within you will guide you in the right direction and help you make the right choice. In those moments, it's reassuring to know other names for the Holy Spirit are Helper and Comforter!

God created you to live a surrendered life so you can enjoy intimacy with him. As you increasingly surrender your life to God, you'll experience the plan he has intended for you from the beginning. It's a life filled with joy, peace, and the power to live for his glory.

ABIDING TRUTH

To experience the fullest blessings of the Spirit-filled life, surrender your will to God's will.

REFLECTION QUESTIONS

1. What does the word "surrender" mean to you? How can this be a potentially difficult concept to grasp/accept?

2. What did Abraham need to surrender to God? What did the disciples need to surrender to God?

3. Can you recall a time when you surrendered something specific to God? If so, how did you see God use your surrendered will to make a way for him to work in your life? If not, is there a time when you should have surrendered something to him? What was the outcome?

4. You began your relationship with Jesus when you admitted you needed him and repented of your sin. How can you move forward with this concept of surrendering? What would it look like to *daily* surrender to his will?

5. Jesus surrendered his life for the church (that's *you!*). What, then, should you be willing to release to God and his will for your life?

6. Contemplate what you currently have not surrendered. Maybe it's a habit, a relationship, or an attitude. What's keeping you from being fully surrendered to Jesus? Give it to him now and ask him to strengthen you through the process.

SONG SUGGESTIONS

"Control" by Tenth Avenue North
"Make Room" by The Church Will Sing/Community Music
"I Surrender All" by Jadon Lavik

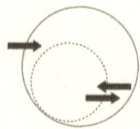

CHAPTER 11

Surrender Your Self-Effort

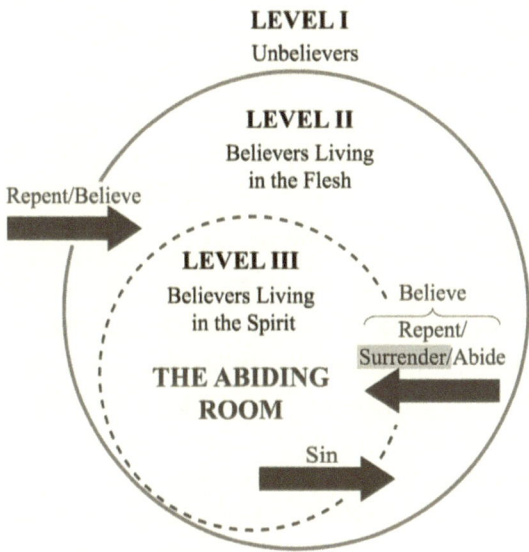

"Come to me, all you who are weary and burdened, and I will give you rest." (Matthew 11:28 NIV)

Do you ever find yourself working to the point of exhaustion? Does it feel like you often check two things off your to-do list, only to find three more have been added, which leaves you feeling overwhelmed? Do you often feel hurried and worried? Do you feel the frustration of doing it well, but knowing it could have been done better? Do you have trouble saying no to the many good things you could do, and as a result, you don't have the energy to do the best thing? Do you find yourself irritated at others who, in your mind, aren't giving 100 percent to the cause?

You're not alone! Many well-intentioned followers of Jesus feel exhausted. We all need to continue to learn to put into practice the reality that following Jesus also means resting in Jesus.

If we know only striving, we are missing out on the abiding life. And if we aren't abiding in Jesus, sadly, we're very likely too familiar with exhaustion. Serving in our own strength will not only wear us out, it will also result in not bearing "much fruit" (John 15:5, 8). Thankfully, when we fully surrender our striving and self-effort, and our hearts are fully connected to Jesus, we can experience rest *and* the bearing of much fruit!

Doesn't that sound contradictory—less effort leading to more fruit? That's because, in many ways, the surrendered life is the opposite of what today's world teaches—if we want better results, we must try harder. This counterintuitive nature of the abiding, Spirit-filled life likely helps explain why a minority of Christians today are experiencing it.

When, however, by faith, we give Jesus our absolute surrender, he graciously reaches out, inviting us to abide in him and receive the fullness of his life and Spirit! We discover Jesus is the way, the truth, and the life to not only eternal salvation, but to contentment in this life as well!

Martha the Tireless Worker

An excellent example of the contrast between abiding in Jesus and relying on self-effort is found in the story of Jesus with Mary and Martha. This is the same Mary we referred to as Mary the Abider of Bethany in chapter 9. Both Mary and her sister Martha were devoted followers of Jesus, but they demonstrated their loyalty in different ways. Let's look again at how Martha put her faith into action.

> As Jesus and his disciples were on their way, he came to a village where a woman named Martha opened her home to him. She had a sister called Mary, who sat at the Lord's feet listening to what he said. **But Martha was distracted by all the preparations** that had to be made. She came to him and asked, "Lord, don't you care that my sister has left me to do the work by myself? Tell her to help me!"

"Martha, Martha," the Lord answered, "you are worried and upset about many things, but few things are needed—or indeed only one. **Mary has chosen what is better,** and it will not be taken away from her." (Luke 10:38–42 NIV)

As we read this story, we need to understand Jesus wasn't condemning Martha. He was fully aware she was working hard out of her desire to serve him in the best way she knew. Yet he was gently instructing her that there was a better way.

Martha was giving it her all. She was fully invested, all in, sold out. She fully recognized Jesus was the Son of God, and she was serving him with all her heart. Because of how she was living out her faith, however, she was missing out on the very best of Jesus in her life. In spite of her passion, she was operating in the flesh and floundering in frustration in Level II. Her focus on the task was distracting her from being teachable. Martha needed to embrace the rest found in abiding in Jesus by surrendering her self-effort.

Jesus was telling her there was rest available in him, and she could put aside all the world's ways of working in her own strength by instead choosing to simply abide in him. Jesus was pointing Martha to abiding *in* him rather than striving *for* him.

Nothing on Our Own

So Jesus said to them, "Truly, truly, I say to you, **the Son can do nothing of his own accord,** but only what he sees the Father doing. For whatever the Father does, that the Son does likewise ... **I can do nothing on my own.**" (John 5:19, 30)

"Do you not believe that I am in the Father and the Father is in me? The words that I say to you **I do not speak on my own authority,** but **the Father who dwells in me does his works.**" (John 14:10)

Jesus described his life as letting God the Father live in and through him. He was not only describing how he lived, but foreshadowing how we are to live—by letting the life of Jesus and the power of the Holy Spirit do in and through us what we cannot do ourselves.

Realizing we are operating in our own strength is not always easy. Similar to Martha, we may have good intentions, but our method is misplaced. While the deeds of the flesh (such as fits of rage, jealousy, and envy) may not describe your typical daily attitude, the fruit of the Holy Spirit (such as joy and peace) may not seem to describe your daily experience either. You may find yourself caught somewhere in the middle.

That middle is the wilderness of Level II living. Do contentment and restful satisfaction seem to elude you as you follow Jesus? Instead of experiencing the freshness of the fruit of the Spirit, do you find yourself fatigued, disillusioned, and, at times, even hopeless? Jesus, who knows your heart, compassionately lets you know he understands. He tenderly instructs you that, regardless of how hard you strive, feeble branches like you and me cannot bear fruit all alone. He says, "The branch cannot bear fruit **by itself**" (John 15:4). Even our best efforts cannot produce the authentic spiritual fruit such as joy and peace that come only from the life of Jesus flowing through us.

Thankfully, it does not have to be this way! Just like Martha, the solution is right next to you—Jesus. He invites you to surrender your reliance on your own strength and instead, rest, trust, and abide in him. He will accept even your smallest act of faith in turning to him, lovingly take your burden upon himself, and walk alongside you.

Three Key Verses Regarding Self-Effort

Three verses taken from three letters written to three churches nicely fit together to encourage us to live by the Holy Spirit and guard against self-effort.

1. Colossians 2:6 tells us, "So then, just as you received Christ Jesus as Lord, continue to live your lives in him" (NIV). You're instructed to *continue* to live your life in Christ Jesus *just as you started*. How did you start your life with Jesus? You received Jesus as Lord. You did not achieve salvation; you received it.

2. How did you receive Jesus and were saved? Ephesians 2:8–9 says, "For by grace you have been saved through faith. And this is not your own doing; it is the gift of God, not a result of works, so that no one may boast." It was by God's grace, through faith, not by your works, that you received Jesus as your Lord and Savior. So, referring back to Colossians 2:6, you are to *continue* to live just as you started—by God's grace, through faith in Jesus, not by your own self-effort (or works).

    The phrase "not by works" means not by your own self-effort. Nevertheless, it is extremely easy for us to slip into doing works by self-effort. Remember, we said self and flesh are essentially the same. While it may not be intentional, it's very common to try doing good works in the flesh. Self-effort is doomed to failure because your no-good flesh cannot bear much fruit. Apart from Jesus, we cannot bear as "much fruit" as we can when we are resting, or abiding, in him.

3. In Galatians 3:3, the apostle Paul addresses the Galatian church in a very direct manner regarding self-effort creeping into their lives. "Are you so foolish? Having begun by the Spirit, are you now being perfected by the flesh?" Paul is saying they started well by receiving the Holy Spirit at salvation, but they've veered off course. They've gone back to the old ways of attempting to do good works and live righteous lives through fleshly efforts. Our intent may be genuine, but, as the Galatian church, too often the means we use to attempt to accomplish it are flawed. Our self-effort to reach the commendable goals of living a life that pleases God is as flawed as our flesh.

Just as you received, not achieved, the gift of salvation, so do you continue to *bear* fruit, not *produce* fruit. The bearing of much fruit is not accomplished through your well-intentioned reliance on yourself. Bearing fruit is accomplished by trusting God, surrendering your self-effort, and letting the Holy Spirit do his work in and through you as you abide in Jesus.

As we connect these three sets of instructions from Paul, we see they give us guidance for how we're to restfully follow Jesus.

Living in the Spirit Vs. the Self-Effort of the Flesh

Too often in our desire to carry out good works, we do so while forgetting the One who inspired us to do them in the first place—Jesus. If we begin with the abiding relationship with Jesus, we can trust the Holy Spirit to guide, direct, and empower us to complete our work.

God created us for a life of purpose that flows from our relationship with him. If our priority becomes more focused on obedience rather than on the relationship, we end up getting less of both. But as we abide in our relationship with Jesus, the Holy Spirit fills us (The Great 2 for 1), and we discover that, not only does the will of God become clearer to us, but the work of God becomes easier for us too.

It's as C.S. Lewis wrote: "Put first things first and we get second things thrown in; put second things first and we lose *both* first and second things."[1] Meaning, if we make our relationship with Jesus our top priority, the good works flow naturally from that relationship. However, if we get things out of order, and thrust forward into attempting to carry out the work in our own strength, we'll experience less of both Jesus and fruit.

Let's compare the difference between attempting to exhibit the fruit of the Spirit through our self-effort and watching it appear naturally as we trust in the power of the Holy Spirit.

First, what does it look like to attempt to live out the fruit of the Spirit in the flesh of self-effort? If you get up in the morning and effectively say to yourself, *Today I'm going to do all I can to be loving and joyful and peaceful and patient and kind and good and faithful and gentle and self-controlled*, you may find (1) at some point you'll stumble, and (2) at some point you'll be exhausted. Why? Because you can't produce those things in the flesh.

The tree of the flesh can produce some meager levels of fruit for a while through self-effort, but eventually a storm will arise that washes away the topsoil and reveals the root of these things is the flesh. You may discover the fruit vanishes, and the deeds of the flesh such as anger, frustration, harsh criticism, and their accompanying fatigue and discouragement appear.

On the other hand, if you get up in the morning and acknowledge, *Lord, I surrender this day to you. You know what is ahead, and I know I can't exhibit the fruit of the Spirit in my own strength, so I am trusting you to do it,* then you can likely count on three things: (1) that the fruit of the Spirit that appears is genuine, (2) at some point you may still stumble, and (3) if at the point of stumbling you quickly acknowledge to Jesus that you messed up and simply start over by surrendering again, you can trust you're back on track, abiding in Jesus.

We *will* mess up, and Jesus will not be surprised because he knows we're in constant training. The Holy Spirit will let us know when we're off-track, but Jesus is not waiting to condemn us. Rather, he's eager to encourage and guide us. At this point, our faithful friend Jesus will gently say to us what he said to the apostle Paul: "My grace is sufficient for you, for my power is made perfect in weakness" (2 Corinthians 12:9).

As you begin each day, isn't it comforting to know that Jesus' grace is constant? His grace is present at the start, the middle, and the end of the day. His grace is present during both your successes and failures. We can rest during the events of the day, knowing it's no longer us attempting to do things for God in our own strength, but Jesus living out his life through us by the Holy Spirit. The secret is to remain connected to Jesus, not to chase perfection.

Life in the Spirit doesn't eliminate the problems and difficulties the fallen world brings into our lives, but if somebody else is doing the work, we won't become nearly as exhausted. By consistently living by the power of the indwelling Holy Spirit, we have Jesus' assurance of bearing much fruit. That's because it's not us striving to produce the fruit; it's Jesus living in us who is doing the work.

Surrendering our self-effort doesn't mean we spend all day napping and expecting things to get done. God didn't save us for leisure and laziness but for kingdom purposes. As we live by the power of the Spirit, we can know what to do and can enthusiastically embrace God's plan for us, experiencing the Spirit's presence and power throughout the day.

Here's how Paul described the transforming work of the gospel in and through him:

> But by the grace of God I am what I am, and his grace toward me was not in vain. On the contrary, **I worked harder than any of them, though it was not I, but the grace of God** that is with me. (1 Corinthians 15:10)

Abide during the process, obey at decision points, and trust God for the results. Over time, you will have fewer and shorter detours in the flesh. And what is even more exciting is that as you increasingly walk in the Spirit, you can be confident that, step-by-step, you are becoming more like Jesus!

Surrendering My Hope in Self

After my dish-smashing incident in 1999, Juli noticed I was no longer angry, harsh, and critical. She was cautiously optimistic that some change had occurred in me. But because she knew I was capable of suppressing my critical nature for short periods of time, she didn't get her hopes up too high. Too many times she'd seen me temporarily will myself to be kind to her after we'd had a long discussion or a fight, only to be disappointed when I returned to my old, harsh, critical, mean self.

We had gone to marriage counseling several times to, as I called it, "Fix Kevin," and I would realize I needed to be kinder and gentler. For a while I would work hard at being that way, but I was still doing it in the flesh, so eventually I would go back to my old ways.

But this time, when I was truly broken by seeing my sin as God saw it, it wasn't self-effort that changed me, it was surrender. I wasn't trying to be kind; I surrendered my right to be angry. I wasn't trying to be gentle; I surrendered my right to be harsh. I wasn't trying to control, suppress, avoid, or eliminate my natural tendencies. I had come to the realization such efforts would eventually prove fruitless, just as they always had, and I would again be headed toward failure.

Although I didn't know God would do such a life-changing work, it began with me surrendering my typical reliance on self-effort in the hope that God would save me from myself. And to his glory, through no self-effort of my own, God filled my emptied heart with his Spirit and began changing our lives.

But that wasn't completely the end of my anger. We went back to biblical marriage counseling a few more times as I began to learn more appropriate behaviors and ways to respond to events that displeased me. More importantly, now I had a better understanding I could control my anger only by the power of the Holy Spirit.

The Love You Had at First

> "I know your deeds, your hard work and your perseverance. I know that you cannot tolerate wicked people, that you have tested those who claim to be apostles but are not, and have found them false. You have persevered and have endured hardships for my name, and have not grown weary. Yet I hold this against you: You have forsaken **the love you had at first.** Consider how far you have fallen! Repent and do the things you did at first." (Revelation 2:2–5 NIV)

Jesus gives us an invitation, saying, "Come to me, all you who are weary" (Matthew 11:28 NIV). Does this describe you? If so, he invites you to surrender your self-effort and rest in him.

Do you remember the freshness of your faith when you first came to Jesus? You knew so little; yet you knew all you needed to know because you knew Jesus. You knew your childlike faith alone was enough. Jesus says everyone, no matter their gifts or experiences, must come to him as a child.

When Jesus calls you friend, he gently invites you to leave behind your self-effort and enjoy his company. Friends don't require our performance; they just enjoy our presence. When you're with your best friend, you're relaxed, rested, smiling, laughing, and enjoying their company. Your friend Jesus is inviting you to throw away your attempts at pleasing him with your self-effort and simply come alongside him and abide.

ABIDING TRUTH

To experience the fullest blessings of the Spirit-filled life, surrender your self-effort and rest in Jesus.

REFLECTION QUESTIONS

1. What are some ways you like to relax? How can you connect those ways to spiritually resting in what Jesus has done for you?

2. How did Jesus describe the contrast in how Martha and Mary lived out their faith?

3. Why is it so difficult for us to grasp the concept of resting in what Christ has already done for us? What societal or cultural norms might stand in the way of this being easy to accept?

4. What are some ways you find yourself getting caught up in self-effort? In what areas are you currently striving when surrender would be a better option?

5. How would you compare abiding in Jesus (listening to the Holy Spirit and doing as he says) versus an attitude of "Let go and let God"?

6. Think about the concept of "do" versus the concept of "done." Jesus died for you, and when he'd done what his Father sent him to do, he said, "It is finished." Take a few minutes to rest in what he's done. Seek him in prayer, and thank him for his sacrifice on the cross.

SUGGESTED SONGS

"Dear God" by Cory Asbury
"Just Be Held" by Casting Crowns
"Truth Be Told" by Matthew West

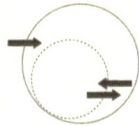

CHAPTER 12

Surrender Your Worldliness

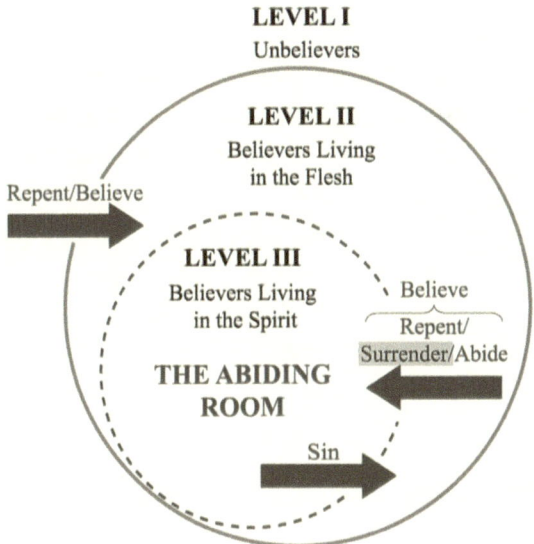

You may remember the Bible passage below from the three types of people described in chapter 2. This passage is used to describe the worldly person living in the flesh in Level II. The NIV translation uses the word "worldly," while the ESV translation uses the word "flesh." That's because the words "worldly" and "flesh" are interchangeable in describing our hearts, as shown in the ESV version below.

> Brothers and sisters, I could not address you as people who live by the Spirit but as people who are still **worldly**—mere infants in Christ. I gave you milk, not solid food, for you were not yet ready for it. Indeed, you are still not ready. You are still **worldly**. For since there is jealousy and quarreling among you, are you not **worldly**?

Are you not acting like mere humans? (1 Corinthians 3:1–4 NIV)

But I, brothers, could not address you as spiritual people, but as people of the **flesh**, as infants in Christ. I fed you with milk, not solid food, for you were not ready for it. And even now you are not yet ready, for you are still of the **flesh**. For while there is jealousy and strife among you, are you not of the **flesh** and behaving only in a human way? (1 Corinthians 3:1–4 ESV)

When we're living in our no-good flesh, the behavior that flows out of our hearts is worldly. When we're living fleshly, worldly lives, we're choosing to live in Level II. We are wandering in the wilderness rather than thriving in the Spirit in the Abiding Room.

Here's the Abiding Room diagram illustrating these verses again:

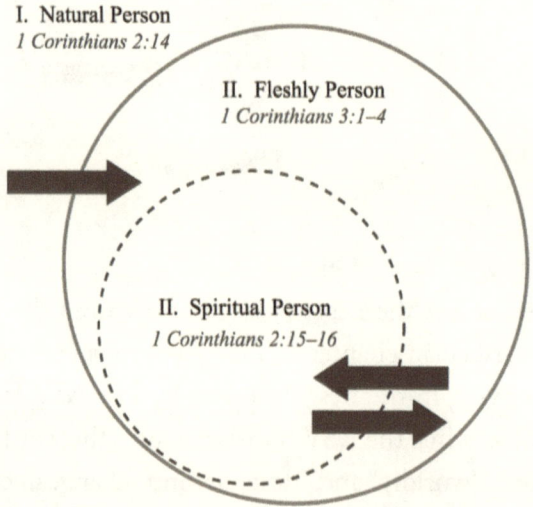

The apostle Paul laments he couldn't even talk to the Corinthian church in spiritual terms because he was too busy addressing the problems of jealousy and quarreling arising from their operating in the flesh. It seems safe to assume Paul would much rather be celebrating the spiritual victories that would have been occurring in their lives if they had been living in the Spirit.

Surrender Your Worldliness

I wonder how many pastors in churches today can relate to Paul's disappointment. They long to teach us the deeper things of Christ, but they are too occupied solving the problems caused by our fleshly, worldly hearts. If it's true that few of us are consistently living in the Spirit, then unfortunately, it is quite likely many pastors can empathize with Paul.

How do we expect to hear from the Holy Spirit when we are choosing to live in a worldly fashion in the flesh? Just as Paul was sad that he couldn't address the deeper spiritual things to the members of this church, today the Holy Spirit is often grieved that he cannot speak to us in a deeper spiritual language because we're living in the flesh.

How, then, do we begin to get out of the rut of worldly, fleshly living? The answer once again lies in the word "surrender."

Surrendering Worldliness

In just two verses, Romans 12:1–2 packs a great deal of instruction regarding surrendering our worldliness. This includes the exciting promise that the blessing of this surrender is to know God's will:

> Therefore, I urge you, brothers and sisters, in view of God's mercy, to **offer your bodies** as a living sacrifice, holy and pleasing to God—this is your true and proper worship. **Do not conform to the pattern of this world** but be transformed by the renewing of your mind. **Then** you will be able to **test and approve what God's will is**—his good, pleasing and perfect will. (Romans 12:1–2 NIV)

This passage instructs us to surrender our whole selves. When the apostle Paul says to offer your body as a sacrifice, he means to give God all of you—your heart, mind, and soul. But also give him your calendar, your checkbook, your ambition, your relationships—*everything*. Give God your complete, absolute surrender. Surrender precedes the outpouring of the blessings of the abiding, Spirit-filled life God the Father has planned for you.

Surrendering your worldliness is an ongoing, lifelong process. It involves developing an attitude of wholehearted release of your life to

God every moment of each day. Expect God to lovingly and repeatedly reveal worldly attitudes of your heart you hadn't noticed. Embrace these new moments of awareness as growth opportunities to yield your heart and your life to Jesus.

These verses instruct you to not be of the world but to be encouraged that by surrendering your life to God, you will be able to discern God's will. Note the word "then." "**Then** you will be able to test and approve what God's will is." The word "then" connects your surrender to the promise you will receive a greater capacity to know God's will.

This passage explains there is a prerequisite to clearly knowing the will of God. This requirement is that you do not align your priorities with what this world says is important. The beginning of the blessing of knowing God's will is the surrender of your worldliness.

The Message paraphrase of Romans 12:1–2 says this for us in everyday language:

> So here's what I want you to do, God helping you: Take your everyday, ordinary life—your sleeping, eating, going-to-work, and walking-around life—and place it before God as an offering. Embracing what God does for you is the best thing you can do for him. Don't become so well-adjusted to your culture that you fit into it without even thinking. Instead, fix your attention on God. You'll be changed from the inside out. Readily recognize what he wants from you, and quickly respond to it. Unlike the culture around you, always dragging you down to its level of immaturity, God brings the best out of you, develops well-formed maturity in you.

When we let go of our desires and passions for the things of this world, we can fix our minds on the things of God. This is part of the gradual process of being "transformed" to be more like Jesus. We change from the Level II fleshly person who craves what this world has to offer to the Level III Spirit-led person whose thinking is guided by the mind of Jesus as described in 1 Corinthians 2:15–16:

The person with the Spirit makes judgments about all things, but such a person is not subject to merely human judgments, for, 'Who has known the mind of the Lord so as to instruct him?' But we have the mind of Christ. (NIV)

Surrendering Your Worldliness—a Recurring Biblical Theme

It's up to us whether we live Level II lives, conformed to the world and living by the flesh, or Level III lives, transformed by God and living by the power of the Holy Spirit. At its heart, worldliness is having any worldly god rather than the one true God. Those worldly gods are idols.

God has always been serious about our choosing him above worldly idols. In the Old Testament, God gave the Israelites the Ten Commandments before they entered the Holy Land, telling them he was to be their first priority.

Here are the first two commandments:

"You shall have no other gods before me." (Exodus 20:3)

"You shall not make for yourself a carved image, or any likeness of anything that is in heaven above, or that is in the earth beneath, or that is in the water under the earth. You shall not bow down to them or serve them, for I the Lord your God am a jealous God, visiting the iniquity of the fathers on the children to the third and the fourth generation of those who hate me, but showing steadfast love to thousands of those who love me and keep my commandments." (Exodus 20:4–6)

Surrender calls on us to align our priorities with those God has for us. One of my favorite verses is a rather obscure one in the Old Testament. The prophet Jonah spoke it while inside the big fish, and it speaks of the enormous cost of loving the things of this world: "Those who cling to worthless idols forfeit the grace that could be theirs" (Jonah 2:8 NIV 1984).

God's grace lavishes us with many, undeserved blessings. However, when our ambition is to love, pursue, and cling to the things of this world, such as recognition, money, and power, we miss out on many of the blessings God intends for us. But when we abandon these temporary worldly trinkets that distract us from God, he pours out his grace on us.

The apostle John describes surrendering our worldliness in the New Testament:

> Do not love the world or the things in the world. If anyone loves the world, the love of the Father is not in him. For all that is in the world—the desires of the flesh and the desires of the eyes and pride of life—is not from the Father but is from the world. And the world is passing away along with its desires, but whoever does the will of God abides forever. (1 John 2:15–17)

Surrender is the remedy to worldliness. To leave behind the wilderness, you must leave behind your worldliness.

Our resources of time, talent, and treasure are truly from God, and we're blessed when we devote them to his plans and purposes. As has been said plenty of times: look at your calendar and your checkbook and you'll know your priorities.

Let's look at those two areas of surrender—time and money.

Surrender Your Worldliness—Time

When you surrender your worldliness, your desire will shift from serving yourself to serving others. You will become a radiant blessing to your community. The needs of those around you are endless. Through community service, you can establish new friendships and learn to better understand the needs of others.

Serving others will broaden your perspective and contribute to your spiritual maturity. You can trust the Holy Spirit to guide you into opportunities to be the hands and feet of Jesus to those who don't yet know him. If you attend church but are still not feeling connected to others, I have a simple, one-word recommendation for you—serve!

Surrendering your worldliness includes ignoring the world's message to be independent, and instead choosing to be engaged in a local church. The world tells us to live for self and make our own way, but God has chosen and gifted us to be part of a local church body.

The Bible puts it this way: "And let us consider how we may spur one another on toward love and good deeds, not giving up **meeting together**, as some are in the habit of doing, but encouraging one another" (Hebrews 10:24–25 NIV).

In today's world of technology, there are plenty of opportunities to fool ourselves into thinking we can be part of a church solely through online worship. But God intends us to be interrelated. When we gather together, we're able to encourage each other, sharpen each other spiritually, and join together in fellowship and service to bless others using our gifts within and outside of the church.

A wonderful part of being connected to Jesus and living the abiding, Spirit-filled life is enjoying all the blessings that arise from fellowship in Jesus' body, the local church. Colossians 1:18 tells us Jesus is the head of the church: "And he is the head of the body, the church."

Some of the most significant experiences of seeing the Holy Spirit at work are when he empowers you in your service within the church. When we're operating in the flesh, we think like the world, asking, *What's in it for me?* On the other hand, when we're living lives surrendered to the Lord, we're looking for ways to serve others, which is what Jesus modeled for us in his earthly ministry.

When our children were young, the temptation for Juli and I was to attend church to be served. After a long week, it can be a challenge just to get everyone fed, dressed, and out the door. But as we relinquished our rights for a leisurely Sunday and began serving, we were blessed in ways we couldn't have predicted. There is no end to how God will bless you in your involvement in serving in small groups, in children's ministries, and other in areas within your church. A surrendered heart is a selfless, serving heart, and a prerequisite for experiencing the fullness of the abiding, Spirit-filled life.

Spirit-filled, Level III followers of Christ are fully engaged in their local church. Regardless of your age, the number of years you've been following Jesus, or your biblical knowledge, God's plan is to utilize the gifts he has given you to bless others. How has God gifted you? Ask your local church leaders how you can identify and utilize your gifts to serve others in your church.

Now, having said all of that, it's worth noting it's entirely possible to serve others in the flesh. The real evidence of being filled, led, and empowered by the Holy Spirit is when your life displays the fruit of the Spirit. It isn't so much that service to others is evidence you are experiencing the abiding, Spirit-filled life, but an *unwillingness* to serve may be a sign that you're not.

Surrender Your Worldliness—Finances

> "Bring the **whole tithe** into the storehouse, that there may be food in my house. **Test me** in this," says the LORD Almighty, "and see if I will not throw open the floodgates of heaven and pour out so much blessing that there will not be room enough to store it." (Malachi 3:10 NIV)

Over the years, I have heard many teachers say this verse is the *only time* in the Bible that God says we should test him. God challenges you to relinquish control of your finances to him, and then watch him keep his promises as he blesses you.

Is this a guarantee against job loss or that the investments in your retirement plan will soar in value? Not at all. It is a statement intended to encourage you to trust God and release your finances to him so you can experience him and the blessings he gives you with your finances.

A wonderful story I heard from a young couple at our church illustrates what surrendering our finances to God can look like. They wanted to begin giving to the church, but, when they sat down and created a budget, their expenses exceeded their income. Nevertheless, God laid it on their hearts to begin giving, so, by faith, they committed to begin regular, generous, monthly giving. Though they couldn't predict it, in the months that followed, unique things kept occurring with their finances that allowed them to balance their budget for the first time! They saw God's faithfulness firsthand!

Surrender Your Worldliness

Everything you have is God's: "The earth is the Lord's, and everything in it, the world, and all who live in it" (Psalm 24:1 NIV). But he has entrusted his resources to you to manage faithfully. And the point is clear—what you do with your finances reveals your priorities. How you use or invest your finances is an accurate picture of what you truly treasure.

The Bible gives this guidance as to the *attitude* of your heart concerning giving when it says:

Each of you should give what you have decided in your heart to give, not reluctantly or under compulsion, for **God loves a cheerful giver.** And God is able to bless you abundantly, so that in all things at all times, having all that you need, you will abound in every good work. (2 Corinthians 9:7–8 NIV)

During my forty years as a financial advisor, I heard countless viewpoints on investments, but one of my favorites comes from a missionary. Jim Elliot was a young man when he and four other missionaries were killed while taking the gospel to a remote village in Ecuador.

After his death, an entry was found in his journal, written several years earlier. It presented a crystal-clear picture of what surrendering our worldliness for eternal purposes looks like. It read: He is no fool who gives what he cannot keep, to gain that which he cannot lose. Jim's life illustrated this principle and serves as a dependable reminder that we are wise to invest our temporary resources of time and money in what is eternal.

When it comes to wisely utilizing the resources God has entrusted to us for kingdom purposes, I prefer the term "investing" rather than "giving." The funds you invest in your church and in ministries are stored for eternity in heaven. As a follower of Jesus, I think it is healthy and appropriate to have an Eternal Kingdom Portfolio mindset. That is, just as you may have (or plan on having) personal investments such as a 401k or IRA for earthly purposes, you can set your mind on investing for eternal purposes. God invites you to join him in his kingdom work so you can experience the joy of participating in activities that will last for eternity.

When you support your church financially, you are part of everything

God is doing there. What you do with your finances matters. God wants you to both be blessed and be a blessing. "Give, and it will be given to you. Good measure, pressed down, shaken together, running over, will be put into your lap. For with the measure you use it will be measured back to you" (Luke 6:38).

Let's be clear, however, we can be generous givers while still in the flesh. It's possible to do the right thing for the wrong reasons. The real evidence of the abiding, Spirit-filled life is, once again, when your life exhibits the fruit of the Spirit. It isn't so much that generous giving is evidence you are experiencing the abiding, Spirit-filled life, but an *unwillingness* to fully release your finances to God is a pretty good sign that you're not.

Surrender, Not Checklists

As we finish these three chapters on surrender, it's possible you are beginning to think this sounds like a checklist of requirements to experience Level III living. There is a fine line between making sure our relationship with Jesus is where it should be and falling into the trap of turning our walk with him into trying to keep a list of dos and don'ts. Following a list of rules is just legalism and religion.

Abiding in Jesus is not about checklists; it's about the condition of your heart. Your heart's condition, as revealed by your attitudes and actions, is of utmost importance so you can experience the abiding, Spirit-filled life in all its fullness. When your heart is fully surrendered to Jesus, the actions we've mentioned flow naturally from it. Moreover, you experience joy and peace from being wholly yielded to God.

ABIDING TRUTH

To experience the fullest blessings of the Spirit-filled life, surrender your worldliness.

REFLECTION QUESTIONS

1. When were you able to move away from an area of your life where worldliness gripped you? Describe what happened.

2. Reread Romans 12:1–2. What stands out to you?

3. We all have a limited amount of time—we can't make more! Consider how you spend your time against the backdrop of worldliness. Then ask yourself, *Do I spend more time abiding, or am I letting "the world" drive my calendar?*

4. *Worldliness* almost sounds like an insult, right? How would you define the term considering the faith Jesus calls us to?

5. First Timothy 6:10 says "For the love of money is a root of all kinds of evil" (NIV). How does this relate to surrendering worldliness? What does society tell us about this principle that scripture either refutes or validates?

6. Take a few minutes to look at your life objectively. Where might the world have crept into your daily routine? If you can identify an area right away, pray now that Jesus will take that out of your path. If nothing springs to mind, ask Jesus to show you where you have an opportunity to be more like him.

SONG SUGGESTIONS

"I Surrender All" by Clay Crosse
"Have It All" by Brian Johnson
"The Motions" by Matthew West

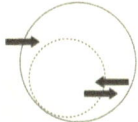

Part Five

HOLY LIVING

CHAPTER 13

God Is Holy

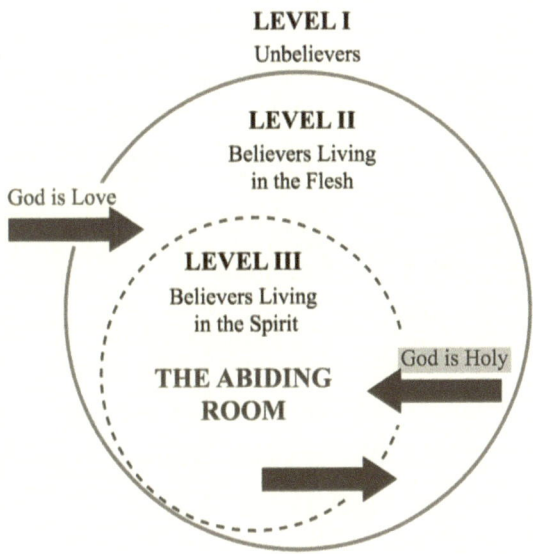

"Be holy, for I am holy." (Leviticus 11:44)

In previous chapters, we've seen four ways the Bible illustrates The 3 Levels of Life. In each case, the innermost circle is the Abiding Room where you experience God's very presence. In chapter 1, we saw the 3 Levels in both the garden of Eden and through the journey of the Israelites. In chapter 2, we explored the 3 Levels through the words of Romans 7 and 8 as well as 1 Corinthians 2 and 3. Each of those illustrations highlighted the significant differences we experience as followers of Jesus depending on whether we are living in the Spirit or the flesh at any given moment.

Now, we'll look at another Biblical illustration of the reality of the

Abiding Room—the temple of God. We'll see how the Abiding Room is actually the holy place of God where we dwell in his presence.

The Definition of Holiness

God describes himself as holy. Holy means to be set apart. It means absolutely pure, perfect, or sacred.

Holiness is the essence of who God is, and because he is holy, he cannot be pleased with anything impure. And since there is nothing good in our flesh (Romans 7:18), God cannot be pleased with his children when we are living in the flesh. But our actions are always pleasing to him when we are filled, led, and empowered by his Holy Spirit. Even in our imperfect, human state, as a loving Father, God is pleased with his children when we're living in the Spirit.

Encountering God's Holy Presence

Throughout the Bible, God repeatedly emphasizes his holiness. When people encounter God's holiness, it is overwhelming and can be terrifying. In the Old Testament book of Leviticus, as God gave Moses and Aaron his regulations for living lives of cleanliness and presenting acceptable offerings to him, he said:

> "For I am the LORD your God. Consecrate yourselves therefore, and **be holy, for I am holy.** You shall not defile yourselves with any swarming thing that crawls on the ground. For I am the LORD who brought you up out of the land of Egypt to be your God. You shall therefore **be holy, for I am holy.**" (Leviticus 11:44–45)

When God was about to save the Israelites from their captivity in Egypt, he appeared to Moses in a burning bush. The voice of God didn't proclaim his love to Moses, but rather God's own holiness. When Moses encountered God, it wasn't a comfortable experience. It was a frightening one, a momentous event that was recounted in the early church more than 1,000 years later in the book of Acts:

Now when forty years had passed, an angel appeared to him in the wilderness of Mount Sinai, in a flame of fire in a bush. When Moses saw it, he was amazed at the sight, and as he drew near to look, there came the voice of the Lord: "I am the God of your fathers, the God of Abraham and of Isaac and of Jacob." **And Moses trembled and did not dare to look.** Then the Lord said to him, "Take off the sandals from your feet, for **the place where you are standing is holy ground.** I have surely seen the affliction of my people who are in Egypt, and have heard their groaning, and I have come down to deliver them. And now come, I will send you to Egypt." (Acts 7:30–34)

Later, Moses asked God to show him his ways so he might know how to find favor in God's sight. God responded by saying his face of unfathomable goodness and holiness could not be looked upon even by Moses, the man of God:

And the Lord said to Moses, "This very thing that you have spoken I will do, for you have found favor in my sight, and I know you by name." Moses said, "Please show me your glory." And he said, "I will make all my goodness pass before you and will proclaim before you my name 'The Lord.' And I will be gracious to whom I will be gracious, and will show mercy on whom I will show mercy. But," he said, "**you cannot see my face, for man shall not see me and live.**" And the Lord said, "Behold, there is a place by me where you shall stand on the rock, and while my glory passes by I will put you in a cleft of the rock, and I will cover you with my hand until I have passed by. Then I will take away my hand, and you shall see my back, but **my face shall not be seen.**" (Exodus 33:17–23)

At the end of the Bible, in the book of Revelation, the apostle John gets a glimpse of Jesus seated on his throne in heaven, and the overwhelming spectacle of heavenly creatures worshiping him day and night without ceasing. They never stop praising God and his holiness:

> "Holy, holy, holy is the Lord God Almighty, who was, and is, and is to come." (Revelation 4:8 NIV)

Ignoring or underestimating the importance of the holiness *of* God leads to a diminished relationship *with* God. The insightful author and thinker of the previous century, A.W. Tozer, writing on God's holiness in his classic book on the nature of God, *The Knowledge of the Holy*, wrote, "Because he [God] is holy, his attributes are holy; that is, whatever we think of as belonging to God must be thought of as holy."[1]

The Tabernacle and Temple of God

The reality that God's holiness sets him apart from sinful mankind is clearly illustrated in physical terms in the architecture of his temple. There, God is distinctly separated from man.

As the Israelites wandered in the desert in the early chapters of the Old Testament, God was with them in the first temple called the tabernacle. The tabernacle could be disassembled and moved when God instructed them.

Many years after the Israelites had entered the Holy Land, Solomon built an extraordinary temple for God in Jerusalem. Solomon's temple was destroyed around 586 BC. Later, the prophet Ezekiel received a vision of another magnificent temple that, to date, has not yet been built. Centuries after Ezekiel's vision, King Herod had another temple built. It was less magnificent than Solomon's temple, and, in AD 70, it was also destroyed.

While people may look at the architecture and marvel at one temple more than others or compare the temple of God with other man-made structures, the true magnificence of any temple is due to God's presence. Physically, one of the commonalities is that each temple consisted of essentially three parts—the outer court, the inner court, and the holy places. God resided in the innermost part of each temple—the holy places. In the Old Testament, only the priests had access to the holy places, and they entered for the purpose of making sacrifices for the sins of the people.

The holy places consisted of both the Holy Place and the Most Holy Place. We will refer to them together as the holy places, which is the term the book of Hebrews uses, as we will see shortly. The Abiding Room is the holy place of God. We can depict the holy places as Level III, as shown in the next diagram:

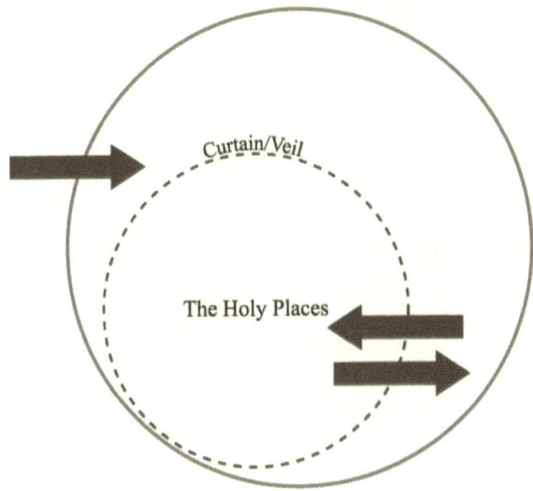

The Glory of God Fills the Temple

In the Old Testament, there are descriptions of special events where the glory of God fills the temple. Each is an overwhelming occasion.

Moses experienced this with the first temple, which was referred to as the tabernacle:

> Then the cloud covered the tent of meeting, and **the glory of the Lord filled the tabernacle.** And Moses was **not able to enter** the tent of meeting **because** the cloud settled on it, and **the glory of the Lord filled the tabernacle.** (Exodus 40:34–35)

When Solomon prayed at the dedication of the temple, whose construction he oversaw, the glory of the Lord again overwhelmed the people as it filled the temple:

As soon as Solomon finished his prayer, fire came down from heaven and consumed the burnt offering and the sacrifices, and **the glory of the Lord filled the temple.** And the priests could not enter the house of the Lord, because **the glory of the Lord filled the Lord's house.** When all the people of Israel saw the fire come down and the glory of the Lord on the temple, they bowed down with their faces to the ground on the pavement and worshiped and gave thanks to the Lord, saying, "For he is good, for his steadfast love endures forever." (2 Chronicles 7:1–3)

The prophet Ezekiel describes a truly awesome experience as the glory of the Lord fills the temple:

"And behold, the glory of the God of Israel was coming from the east. And the sound of his coming was like the sound of many waters, and the earth shone with his glory. And the vision I saw was just like the vision that I had seen when he came to destroy the city, and just like the vision that I had seen by the Chebar canal. And I fell on my face. As the glory of the Lord entered the temple by the gate facing east, the Spirit lifted me up and brought me into the inner court; and behold, **the glory of the Lord filled the temple."** (Ezekiel 43:2–5)

God's presence, power, majesty, and holiness are in his temple and are apparent to all who encounter him. Throughout history, God's glory filling the temple was a staggering revelation of God to man.

Jesus Made a Way into the Holy Places

Much as God dramatically revealed the salvation of mankind through the parting of the Red Sea, he revealed a new relationship with mankind through the profound tearing of the temple veil that separated us from the holy places:

From noon until three in the afternoon darkness came over all the land ... And when Jesus had cried out again in a loud voice, he

God Is Holy

gave up his spirit. **At that moment the curtain of the temple was torn in two from top to bottom.** The earth shook, the rocks split and the tombs broke open. (Matthew 27:45, 50–52 NIV)

God tore the veil in a way only he could—from top to bottom—at the exact moment Jesus died for mankind's sins. The tearing of the veil symbolized the death of Jesus made a way we could enter into the presence of God. By Jesus' blood, a new covenant (agreement) with mankind had begun, and we can now have a wonderful abiding fellowship with God through Jesus.

In the Old Testament, the priests entered the holy places to repeatedly make sacrifices on behalf of the people for their sin. But now, because of Jesus' perfect sacrifice on the cross for your sin, he has made a way for you to enter into fellowship with your Holy God.

> But when Christ appeared as a high priest of the good things that have come, then through the greater and more perfect tent (not made with hands, that is, not of this creation) **he entered once for all into the holy places,** not by means of the blood of goats and calves but by means of his own blood, thus securing an eternal redemption. For if the blood of goats and bulls, and the sprinkling of defiled persons with the ashes of a heifer, sanctify for the purification of the flesh, how much more will the blood of Christ, who through the eternal Spirit offered himself without blemish to God, purify our conscience from dead works to serve the living God. (Hebrews 9:11–14)

There is no more need for a physical temple where priests make sacrifices for your sins. Jesus' death means you can experience intimate fellowship with God without the need for a physical temple:

> For Christ has entered, not into **holy places** made with hands, which are copies of the true things, but into heaven itself, now to appear in the presence of God on our behalf. **Nor was it to offer**

himself repeatedly, as the high priest enters the **holy places** every year with blood not his own, for then he would have had to suffer repeatedly since the foundation of the world. But as it is, he has appeared **once for all** at the end of the ages to put away sin by the sacrifice of himself. (Hebrews 9:24–26)

Jesus made a way for you to enter into the holy places that were once off-limits to ordinary people like us. He made a way for you to enter that no longer requires the blood of animals. You can walk through this door that is made possible by his blood.

Because God is holy, however, the presence of any sin must be addressed. The wonderous reality of entering the holy places of precious intimacy with Jesus exists by God's grace but requires your humble submission. You may approach the throne of Jesus having first responded in faith by confession and repentance of any sin the Holy Spirit reveals to you. The writer of Hebrews describes your confident entry into God's presence this way:

> Therefore, brothers, since we have confidence to enter the holy places by the blood of Jesus, by the new and living way that he opened for us through the curtain, that is, through his flesh, and since we have a great priest over the house of God, let us draw near with a true heart in full assurance of faith, with our hearts sprinkled clean from an evil conscience and our bodies washed with pure water. (Hebrews 10:19–22)

Fear Has Been Replaced by Joy

The Abiding Room *is* the holy places. Jesus has made the holy rooms once reserved exclusively for priests the new Abiding Room for ordinary people like you and me! Jesus has made a way so that the holy places even priests once entered with fear can now be entered by all God's children with joy. Fear has been replaced by joy!

The reality of this new privilege gets even better. Jesus sets no time limit on how long you can remain in his holy presence. It is up to you. As long as you abide and obey, you can remain in the joy of the Lord:

> "**If you keep my commandments, you will abide in my love,** just as I have kept my Father's commandments and abide in his love. These things I have spoken to you, that **my joy may be in you,** and **that your joy may be full.**" (John 15:10–11)

Praise to the name of Jesus, who made a way for you to both enter into and remain in the joy of his presence and the presence of his joy!

You Are the Temple of the Holy Spirit

> Do you not know that **you are God's temple** and that **God's Spirit dwells in you?** (1 Corinthians 3:16)

> Do you not know that **your bodies are temples of the Holy Spirit, who is in you,** whom you have received from God? You are not your own; you were bought at a price. Therefore honor God with your bodies. (1 Corinthians 6:19–20 NIV)

Beginning with Pentecost in the New Testament, God's Holy Spirit took up residence in a new temple without walls—the hearts of Jesus' followers. Once again, it's not the externals of God's temple that matter, but to what extent the occupant of the house—the indwelling, almighty God—is put on display.

In the verses above, twice Paul teaches the Corinthian church that they are the temples of God. In each case, Paul is reminding them of their great privilege of being indwelt by the Spirit of God and of the accompanying high calling it entails. The Spirit of God is holy, and as a result, the church at Corinth, as well as you and me today, are called to lives that are pure and devoted to God.

When you were first saved and the Holy Spirit made your heart his permanent home, he didn't move into an immaculate residence. He moved in with the mandate from God to gently and intentionally begin a cleaning project that will last your entire lifetime. It's up to you as to when you are obedient to actively carry out the Holy Spirit's instructions. You get to choose when to start and how deep you're willing to clean. You can procrastinate, or you can quickly initiate changes to begin experiencing the joy and peace that accompanies the filling of the Holy Spirit.

Know for certain that, even when you are living in the flesh, the Holy Spirit is still living in you. And be encouraged that the entire time you are taking actions of obedience, Jesus is smiling. He is watching in delight as you are becoming the person he's always known you will be and as your heart continually becomes a more beautiful palace for the Holy Spirit to reside in.

> If the Spirit of him who raised Jesus from the dead dwells in you, he who raised Christ Jesus from the dead will also give life to your mortal bodies through **his Spirit who dwells in you.** (Romans 8:11)

Today, God is still glorified when his temple is filled with the Holy Spirit, but now that temple is you! Every follower of Jesus is the temple of God and indwelt with the person of the Holy Spirit. It is God's desire that you, your body, and your life put his glory on display. This is accomplished when you are filled with the Holy Spirit. As you abide in Jesus, God's temple is being continuously filled with the Holy Spirit—The Great 2 for 1.

Pursue Holiness

> **Pursue** peace with all people, **and the holiness** without which no one will see the Lord. (Hebrews 12:14 NASB)

Think about how, so many years ago, great men of God such as Moses, Solomon, and Ezekiel were overwhelmed by the glory of God filling the temple in the Old Testament. Isn't it almost incomprehensible that as a follower of Jesus you have the same Holy Spirit residing in your heart? Isn't it astounding you have access to the very same power every minute of every day through the indwelling Holy Spirit? What an immense gift the gracious God of the universe has given you as his child in the person of the Holy Spirit!

No one in this lifetime becomes and remains entirely holy, but God tells us to *pursue* holiness. Since God alone is holy, when we desire to be holy as God is holy, our only option is to pursue God himself. This is a lifelong pursuit. But just as a loving, earthly father takes joy in running with his small child and letting himself be caught, so, too, does your heavenly Father. In his love and grace, when you wholeheartedly pursue him, God takes joy in letting you "catch" him— and then filling you with his Holy Spirit!

ABIDING TRUTH

Jesus has made a way for you to enter
into the presence of the Holy God
by making your body the temple of his Holy Spirit.

REFLECTION QUESTIONS

1. Think of a time when you experienced the presence of the holiness of God. What did that feel like?

2. Why should we, like Moses, recognize God's holiness as part of our growing relationship with him?

3. How does the tearing of the curtain at Jesus' death relate to the holiness of God? What impact did this have on how Jesus' followers would interact with God from this point forward?

4. The dwelling place of God's Spirit changed as fear gave way to joy. Why was this change necessary for us to move into a more intimate relationship with God?

5. What are some ways you could pursue the holiness God asks for?

SONG SUGGESTIONS

"Holy Forever" by Chris Tomlin
"Revelation Song" by Phillips, Craig and Dean
"Ancient Gates" by Brooke Fraser Ligertwood
"Temple" by Brandon Lake

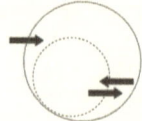

CHAPTER 14

Repentance

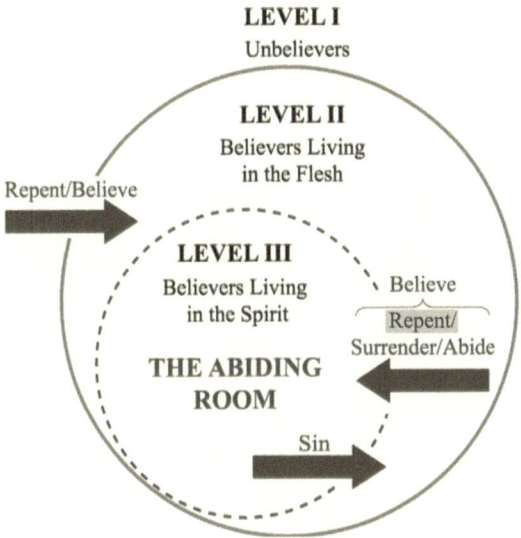

Or do you presume on the riches of his kindness and forbearance and patience, not knowing that God's kindness is meant to lead you to repentance? (Romans 2:4)

In this chapter, we will discuss repentance for followers of Jesus after salvation. Repentance relates to God's holiness and your ongoing choice to live in the flesh or in the Spirit at any given moment.

The word "Repent" is now shaded in the diagram.

Repentance Defined

What is repentance? Repentance means having a change of heart and mind that causes us to turn from going our own way and instead go God's way. It means turning from our sin to God.

Restoration Not Condemnation

> There is therefore now **no condemnation** for those who are in Christ Jesus. For the law of the Spirit of life **has set you free** in Christ Jesus from the law of sin and death. (Romans 8:1–2)

While God's unconditional love means we will never lose our relationship with him, repentance brings us back into the fullness of that relationship. It's part of God's plan for our continual, full, relational restoration with him. It does not lead to punishment or condemnation, but rather to restoration!

Repentance, like surrender, is another condition required for believers to experience the deeper, abiding fellowship with Jesus. Our sin is a barrier that keeps us from abiding. Repentance is the remedy to this barrier. Having repented of known sin, we can abide in Jesus and thus be filled with the Spirit.

> And I pray that you, being rooted and established in love, may have power, together with all the Lord's holy people, to grasp how wide and long and high and deep is the love of Christ, and to know this love that surpasses knowledge—**that you may be filled to the measure of all the fullness of God.** (Ephesians 3:17–19 NIV)

As followers of Jesus, we need to continually renew our minds. Repentance is part of the transformational thinking that brings transformational living. God lovingly accepts our repentance when we acknowledge our sin. When sin is present, God is always eagerly awaiting our repentance. It is certain that when you repent, God will forgive you!

God Is Holy

Let's briefly review the diagram that shows God is *both* love and holy.

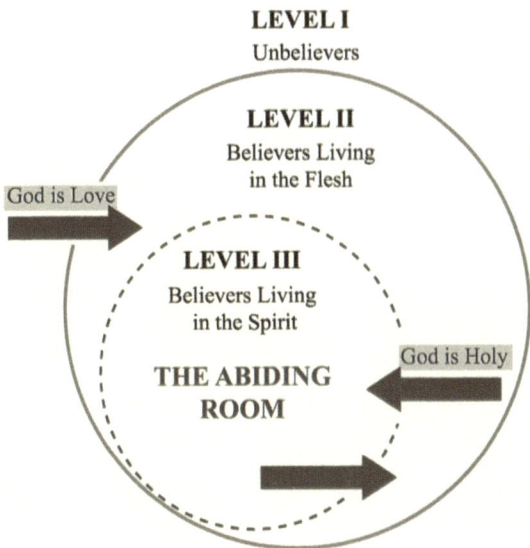

Once more, it is important to understand God is holy. And again, the word "holy" means set apart or sacred. God is without any trace of sin or evil.

As we learned in chapter 1, when Adam and Eve sinned, they could no longer live in the garden of Eden. A barrier was placed between God and all humankind. Why? Because God is holy, and as a result, there were consequences for man's sin.

Because God is holy and because you are his beloved child, he cannot be pleased when you sin. When we sin, it negatively impacts our relationship with him. While God's love is unconditional, his pleasure is conditional, because he is holy:

> "For I am the LORD your God. Consecrate yourselves therefore, and **be holy for I am holy** ... For I am the LORD who brought you up out of the land of Egypt to be your God. You shall therefore **be holy, for I am holy**." (Leviticus 11:44–45)

God's Holiness Reveals Our Sin

Isaiah 6 tells of the prophet Isaiah's dramatic encounter with God's holiness:

"In the year that King Uzziah died I saw the Lord sitting upon a throne, high and lifted up; and the train of his robe filled the temple. Above him stood the seraphim. Each had six wings: with two he covered his face, and with two he covered his feet, and with two he flew. And one called to another and said: '**Holy, holy, holy** is the Lord of hosts; the whole earth is full of his glory!'" (Isaiah 6:1–3)

There is no hiding our sin from our all-knowing God. When we seek God, his character and his holiness are revealed to us. His holiness reveals to us any sin that is present. This is when we see ourselves as God sees us. Isaiah experienced the conviction of sin in his encounter with God's holy presence:

"And the foundations of the thresholds shook at the voice of him who called, and the house was filled with smoke. **And I said: 'Woe is me! For I am lost; for I am a man of unclean lips,** and I dwell in the midst of a people of unclean lips; **for my eyes have seen the King,** the Lord of hosts!'" (Isaiah 6:4–5)

When the presence and work of the Holy Spirit convicts us of the presence of sin in our lives, our correct response is repentance. We repent because of who God is. He is holy. God desires the best for us, and that means he leads us to repentance.

Even in repentance, our depraved hearts will always fall short of God's holiness. Thankfully, his grace bridges the gap from our repentance to his holy presence. Isaiah experienced this firsthand when God reached out and restored him:

"Then one of the seraphim **flew to me,** having in his hand a burning coal that he had taken with tongs from the altar. And he touched my mouth and said: 'Behold, this has touched your lips; **your guilt is taken away, and your sin atoned for.**'" (Isaiah 6:6–7)

God's Best for You Leads You to Repentance

> **Your sorrow led you to repentance.** For you became sorrowful as God intended and so were not harmed in any way by us. Godly sorrow brings repentance that leads to salvation and leaves no regret, but worldly sorrow brings death. (2 Corinthians 7:9–10 NIV)

Note how this passage distinguishes godly sorrow from worldly sorrow. Worldly sorrow does not lead to repentance. We can be sorry we got caught in sin or that we are experiencing the consequences of sin, without repenting.

Godly sorrow brings repentance, not merely regret. Godly sorrow leads us to genuine repentance not merely because it will relieve or reduce our pain but because we see our sin as God sees it. Godly sorrow produces a deep conviction and a sincere hatred toward sin because it is a detestable offense toward our Holy God.

Disconnecting by Disobedience

> So whoever knows the right thing to do and fails to do it, for him it is sin. (James 4:17)

In the next diagram, the word "Sin" is highlighted on the out arrow.

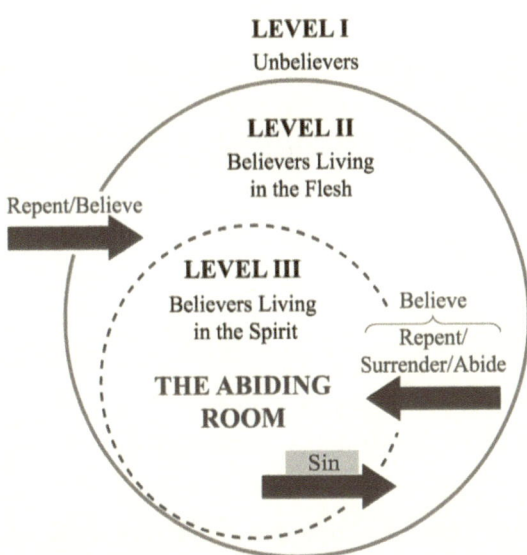

Sin impacts our abiding relationship with God. When you sin, God still loves you because he is love, and you are his beloved child. But God cannot be pleased with your sin because he is holy. When you receive instruction from the Lord through his Word or his Spirit's promptings, and you know what to do but choose to disobey, that is sin. A stubborn refusal to repent leads to the loss of the fullness of the blessing of abiding in Jesus and being filled with the Holy Spirit.

> Everyone who makes a practice of sinning also practices lawlessness; sin is lawlessness. You know that he appeared in order to take away sins, and in him there is no sin. **No one who abides in him keeps on sinning.** (1 John 3:4–6)

As we saw earlier, sin grieves the person of the Holy Spirit and quenches his power, as described in Ephesians 4:30 and 1 Thessalonians 5:19. And though the Holy Spirit has come to dwell in you forever, sin creates uncleanliness that diminishes the fullness of your intimacy with Jesus.

There's more at stake than simply whether or not you will repent. It's a choice of whether or not you will abide in Jesus and be filled with the Spirit. All the wonderful blessings of the abiding, Spirit-filled life we have examined in previous chapters are available when we acknowledge our sin and repent. The decision to repent carries with it the choice to either be part of the minority who generally reside within the Abiding Room or among the majority of Christians living primarily outside of the Abiding Room.

> Make every effort to live in peace with everyone and to **be holy; without holiness** no one will see the Lord. (Hebrews 12:14 NIV)

Stated in absolute terms, if you won't repent, it displeases God. If you refuse to repent, you cannot expect to fully abide and thus be filled with the Holy Spirit. Our refusal to repent is a personal choice to not be filled with the Holy Spirit. It's a choice to live a Level II life rather than experience the full abundance of a harmonious relationship with God in

Repentance

Level III, Spirit-filled living. Yes, God's love, mercy, and grace remain, but so does his holiness.

Is it worth the loss of God's full favor and blessing to stubbornly refuse to repent of known sin?

The "Continual" Way of Living

Just as with any other relationship, our relationship with Jesus is constantly changing. In John 15:5, when Jesus said, "Abide in me," he was in essence saying, "Remain in *continual* fellowship with me." Ephesians 5:18 essentially says, "being *continually* filled with the Spirit." Similarly, Colossians 2:6 says, "So then, just as you received Christ Jesus as Lord, **continue** to live your lives in him" (NIV).

This principle of continuity applies to repentance as well. Walking in the Spirit is a life of ongoing repentance. Repentance is not only how you were saved initially; it's also how you are renewed continually.

As he prepared the way for Jesus' ministry, John the Baptist said, "Bear fruit in **keeping with repentance**" (Matthew 3:8). You began your walk with Jesus by repenting. The good work God started in you carries on within you as his grace continues to lead you to repentance.

In his book, *Repentance, The First Word of the Gospel*, Richard Owen Roberts says, "When a Christian grows careless about repentance, sin and self begin to crowd back into the life, and moral and spiritual decline set in as God demonstrates his displeasure by withdrawing more and more of his manifest presence. When true repentance occurs, a moral and spiritual recovery is made as God returns in refreshing power. If one lives in perpetual repentance as one ought, neither the decline nor the renewal occurs, but rather a steady upward movement is discernable. But alas, few live in consistent repentance, and thus an erratic lifestyle characterizes most professed Christians."[1]

Confession and Repentance Together

> If we say we have no sin, we deceive ourselves, and the truth is not in us. If we **confess our sins**, he is faithful and just to **forgive us** our sins and to **cleanse us** from all unrighteousness. (1 John 1:8–9)

Confessing means agreeing with God about your sin. Confession precedes repentance. It's easy to get caught up in the cycle of "sin, confess, sin, confess" but never come to repentance. If you keep repeating the same sins in your life, perhaps it's because you're going the same way and haven't turned around. It's quite possible to agree with God that you're going the wrong way (confession) without turning around (repentance).

To experience the abiding, Spirit-filled life, when you sin, the only thing that will get you going back in God's direction is the life-changing, heartfelt turnaround of repentance. When the Holy Spirit reveals your sin, you need to agree with God that what he says is true, and turn back to him by repenting.

Jesus Welcomes Repentance

Jesus is always giving you an open invitation to repent when sin is present so you can experience the fullness of his presence and blessings. It is his desire for you to become more like him, so he gave you the Holy Spirit to reveal your sin so you will turn from it.

Let's look back at the Last Supper when Jesus was with his disciples and described the abiding relationship. First, he described the people in the relationship—the Father as the Vinedresser, Jesus as the true Vine, and his followers as the branches. Then he told the disciples they were already clean. Next, he said, "Abide in me," and began describing the blessings of bearing much fruit, answered prayer, etc., that flow from the abiding relationship with him. The disciples were attentive listeners and learners as Jesus spoke.

What if instead of being submissive, obedient, teachable, and attentive, the disciples were constantly debating Jesus on what he was teaching them? What if each time he taught them something, they were saying things such as, "No, I disagree. I think you're wrong. Here's what I think."? Do you think Jesus, the Son of God, would have ignored their resistance and continued to share with them the intimacy of the abiding life if they were exhibiting those types of attitudes toward his teaching?

Or, what if while Jesus was speaking, they were all sitting around the table looking at pornographic drawings? What if they were sexually involved with women who weren't their wives? Do you think Jesus would have ignored these sinful behaviors? It's more likely he would have spoken to them as he often spoke to the crowds following him—speaking direct truths so they might understand and make important adjustments in their lives. It's much more likely he would have dealt with their sin before he invited them to abide in him.

Rest assured that when you mess up, Jesus is never looking to harshly say "Gotcha!" Far from it. Instead, he is always there to catch you and gently say "Don't worry. I gotcha." He stands there with open arms, ready to embrace you with his love, grace, mercy, and forgiveness.

The Restoration of Joy Arising from Repentance

> Restore to me the joy of your salvation and grant me a willing spirit, to sustain me. (Psalm 51:12 NIV)

Can you wholeheartedly say you're experiencing the joy of the Lord? The beginning of the restoration of the joy of your salvation, as King David asked for in Psalm 51, is one U-turn away. Repentance triggers an outpouring of God's grace and mercy that brings the joy of the restoration of a right relationship with God.

It is worth noting that while repentance is turning to go in the right direction, typically it won't immediately bring you to your destination. Any journey begins by taking a first step in the right direction, and you will need others to accompany and help you.

Long-term ingrained sin patterns and addictions take time to overcome. You may need to talk to a pastor, seek counseling, or enroll in a program specifically designed to assist you in your commitment to change.

As you consider the truths of repentance, which can be an uncomfortable process, don't get discouraged. Don't stop! Keep going—this is the process that leads to blessing! This leads to God's best for you and all that he has in store for you.

God's Word reminds you of this:

God disciplines us for our good, in order that **we may share in his holiness.** No discipline seems pleasant at the time, but painful. Later on, however, **it produces a harvest of righteousness and peace** for those who have been trained by it. (Hebrews 12:10–11 NIV)

"The Lord your God is with you, the Mighty Warrior who saves. He will take great delight in you **in his love he will no longer rebuke you, but will rejoice over you with singing.**" (Zephaniah 3:17 NIV)

Search Me, O God

Do you long to have the blessings of intimacy with Jesus poured out on you richly as the previous verses remind us? Do you long for the regeneration and daily renewal of the fullness of the Holy Spirit? The awareness of any sin in your life is merely a short prayer away. It simply involves asking your merciful heavenly Father to search your heart and open your eyes, mind, and heart to any sin that exists.

I encourage you to meditate and pray Psalm 139:23–24 below with sincerity right now. Go before God and genuinely ask him to search your heart:

Search me, God, and know my heart; test me and know my anxious thoughts. See if there is any offensive way in me, and lead me in the way everlasting. (Psalm 139:23–24 NIV)

God sees your heart as clearly as you see the words on this page. What is the Holy Spirit saying to you at this moment? Did he bring to mind something you need to do? Did he bring to mind someone you need to go to?

Right now, you might be squirming as you think about what it might cost you to fully follow Jesus and repent of your sin. If I were sitting across from you, I'd do everything to keep you from squirming out of this. There's too much at stake. You have too much to gain! Don't let your pride stand in the way of you making a spiritual U-turn. Take action. Turn around now so you are heading in the right direction. Repentance restores, refreshes, and revives.

Listen to what God is saying to you and obey. The rewards await!

To him who is **able to keep you from stumbling** and to present you **before his glorious presence without fault and with great joy**—to the only God our Savior be glory, majesty, power and authority, through Jesus Christ our Lord, before all ages, now and forevermore! Amen. (Jude 24–25 NIV)

ABIDING TRUTH

Because God is holy,
to experience the fullest blessings of the Spirit-filled life,
repent of all known sin.

REFLECTION QUESTIONS

1. What does it mean to you to repent? What does repentance look like?

2. To repent of sin, we must first confess. What about that is difficult for you? Is it easier to confess to Jesus than to another person? Why or why not?

3. Repentance is to "turn away" and follow a new or different path. What can get in the way of repentance leading to real change in your life?

4. We are led to repentance by God's kindness. How is this different from repentance born of fear? In what ways is God's way more effective?

5. What do you need to repent of today? Start by identifying it and telling Jesus you agree with him that it is sin. Ask him to help you repent of this sin and walk in a new direction. Then give him praise for his loving-kindness!

SONG SUGGESTIONS

"As You Find Me" by Hillsong United
"Point to You" by We Are Messengers
"Holy" by Nichole Nordeman

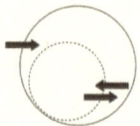

CHAPTER 15

Forgiveness

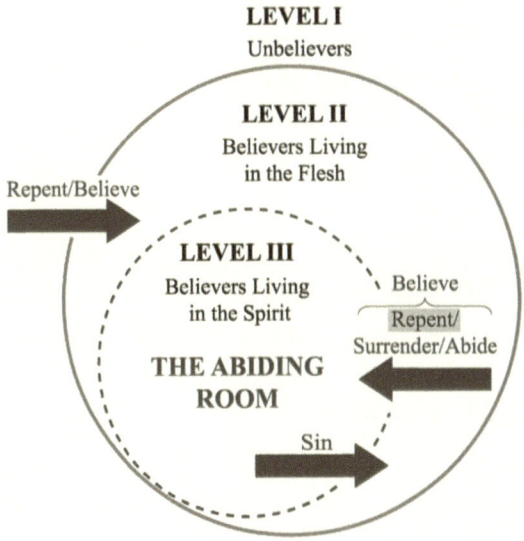

And do not grieve the Holy Spirit of God, with whom you were sealed for the day of redemption. Get rid of all bitterness, rage and anger, brawling and slander, along with every form of malice. Be kind and compassionate to one another, forgiving each other, just as in Christ God forgave you. (Ephesians 4:30–32 NIV)

Perhaps you've had the experience of receiving a notice of a gathering, reunion, wedding, or some other event you would like to attend, but your mind quickly jumped to the thought, *"Oh no!* THAT PERSON *who did* THAT THING *to me will be there!"* Instead of being excited about attending the event and seeing family and friends, you begin fretting about having to be in the same room with THAT PERSON. Have you ever felt like that? I know I have.

We Are Commanded to Forgive

We have looked at many aspects of how we can experience the abiding, Spirit-filled life. Now let's look at an important, common hindrance to experiencing the fullest blessings of Level III living—unforgiveness. It falls within the category of repentance, but it's addressed separately and saved for last because it merits special attention.

Jesus commands us to forgive each other. In Matthew 6:14–15, he said, "For **if you forgive** other people when they sin against you, **your heavenly Father will also forgive you.** But **if you do not forgive** others their sins, **your Father will not forgive your sins**" (NIV).

Unforgiveness is a difficult issue that comes in many forms and often lingers for years. It digs deep into our hearts and is tough to get out permanently, often reappearing suddenly as a major barrier to Spirit-filled living. Is anyone immune to its impact?

We have *all* had people do things to us that hurt deeply. Perhaps you've had some things done to you that are horrendous. But the Word of God is consistent—the path to freedom and the overflowing blessing of Jesus is forgiveness in your heart.

Ephesians 4:30–32 at the beginning of the chapter shows us the connection between unforgiveness and grieving the Holy Spirit. When we have unforgiveness in our hearts, it grieves the person of the Holy Spirit. When in our flesh we choose to not forgive, we are also choosing to forfeit the fullness of the blessings of abiding in Jesus. The lack of love in our hearts brings with it a loss of joy and peace not just toward the unforgiven person, but across our entire lives.

Jesus instructs us to love each other as he loves us. Therefore, if we choose not to forgive another person, it is direct disobedience to his command. Even partial disobedience is disobedience, and disobedience is sin. As we've seen, going all the way back to Adam in the garden of Eden, sin separates us from the abiding relationship with God. It was that way in the garden, and it is that way today.

Experiencing the fullest measure of fruit bearing Jesus described when we are abiding in him is negated when the poison of unforgiveness resides in us. God, however, will bless your obedience to repent of unforgiveness with the power to live in freedom that cannot be experienced otherwise.

Forgiveness, then, is the obedience that comes about after we confess (agree with God about our sin) and repent (turn from our sin to God). Obedience to forgive others can take us from Level II to Level III living.

Be assured, God still loves you unconditionally and can choose to bless you even if you don't forgive. It's not that God will abandon you if you are unrepentant, but he longs to pour out even greater blessings to those whose hearts have been made clean by repenting of their unforgiveness.

Unforgiveness in Our Lives

The reasons for unforgiveness are extensive and may include when someone:

- ignored you
- continually disappointed you
- continually criticized you
- snubbed you
- failed to appreciate your efforts
- claimed your work as theirs
- cheated you
- excluded you from their group
- used you and then dumped you
- fired you
- lied to you or about you
- gossiped about you
- harmed you financially
- harmed you verbally
- harmed you physically
- harmed you sexually

Of course, this is not a complete list. Someone may have done some other awful thing to you. But whatever the offense, our unforgiveness can often reveal itself in a desire to see the offender punished. We may fear they'll get away with it and even think of ways to get even with them. This may manifest itself in actions such as ignoring them, being rude to them, telling others about their offenses, or other forms of revenge.

God, however, is clear that he is in charge of repaying them for their sin:

> Repay no one evil for evil, but give thought to do what is honorable in the sight of all. If possible, so far as it depends on you, live peaceably with all. Beloved, never avenge yourselves, but leave it to the wrath of God, for it is written, "Vengeance is mine, I will repay, says the Lord." To the contrary, "if your enemy is hungry, feed him; if he is thirsty, give him something to drink; for by so doing you will heap burning coals on his head." Do not be overcome by evil, but overcome evil with good. (Romans 12:17–21)

Doesn't knowing that God is aware of their sin, of how it hurt you, and that he promises to deal with them in his way and timing give you greater freedom to forgive them?

It's possible THAT PERSON may be unaware they've harmed you. You may have even discussed the situation with them, and they downplayed or refused to acknowledge their offense. But your forgiveness cannot be dependent upon their viewpoint and actions, because those are out of your control. What is within your control is your ability to choose to give up your devotion to your unforgiveness and allow the Spirit of God to empower you to forgive them.

Forgiveness doesn't mean forgetting what was done to you. It doesn't necessarily result in reconciliation. It may or may not result in trust being restored in the person who harmed you. It is possible to forgive and still wrestle with the emotions of having been hurt. The process of forgiving may very naturally lead to feelings of anger, mourning, and sorrow.

Jesus understands the heartache you feel from the wrongs done to you. While Jesus forgave everyone who sinned against him, he still felt pain as a result of the hurtful actions of others:

> "He was despised and rejected by men; a man of sorrows, and acquainted with grief." (Isaiah 53:3)

God recognizes you will feel pain from the unkind or hostile actions of others and is always available to let you unload your burdens on him. He promises to be with you and comfort you in the midst of your pain:

"Blessed are those who mourn, for they shall be comforted." (Matthew 5:4)

Again, it's possible—and reasonable—to mourn, grieve, and feel anger as you process your unforgiveness. Ultimately, what you choose to do with those emotions is what matters to God.

In the never-ending spiritual battle going on in your heart between your flesh and the Holy Spirit, your flesh may continue to remind you of the unjust actions of THAT PERSON. Do not be discouraged—this is a battle you can win by the power of the Spirit within you.

The Holy Spirit, whom Jesus sent as a Counselor to indwell your heart, continues his work to bring you to full spiritual maturity as you become more like Jesus. The Holy Spirit will minister to you as you take steps to forgive. He will guide you in the same way as Jesus always has—in love. Freedom from the burden of unforgiveness is available to you if you choose to be obedient to his leading.

Love and Forgiveness Go Together

On his last night before the cross, as he introduced and connected the abiding life with the upcoming arrival of the Holy Spirit, Jesus also tied love and obedience together. Jesus knew unforgiveness would be a problem. And he knew we can't be both unforgiving and loving toward someone at the same time. So just before he began laying out the abiding, Spirit-filled life at the Last Supper in John 14–16, he spoke about loving each other:

"**A new command** I give you: **Love one another.** As I have loved you, so **you must love one another.** By this, everyone will know that you are my disciples, if you love one another." (John 13:34–35 NIV)

"If you love me, you will **keep my commandments.**" (John 14:15)

> **"If you keep my commandments, you will abide** in my love, just as I have kept my Father's commandments and **abide** in his love. These things I have spoken to you, that my joy may be in you, and that your joy may be full. This is **my commandment,** that you **love one another** as I have loved you." (John 15:10–12)

Jesus connected abiding in him with loving others. He didn't say, "Love and forgive *if* …" or "Love and forgive *except* …" or "Love and forgive *when* …" Jesus never said to love and forgive others *if* they acknowledge they are wrong, or *if* they say they are sorry, or *if* they make things right. He simply said, "Love one another."

Love and unforgiveness cannot co-exist. If we won't forgive someone, we're unable to love them as Jesus loves us. When we choose to not forgive, we're also choosing to disobey Jesus' instructions regarding loving others. He said:

> We love because he first loved us. If anyone says, "I love God," and hates his brother, he is a liar; for he who does not love his brother whom he has seen cannot love God whom he has not seen. And this commandment we have from him: whoever loves God must also love his brother. (1 John 4:19–21)

Without question, forgiving others is easier said than done. You may need to talk to a pastor or leader in your church, a good friend, or a biblical counselor. It may be a process that takes weeks, months, or years. It may pop up again in your heart and need to be revisited. But regardless of the challenges, pursue whatever actions are necessary to rid yourself of unforgiveness.

> **Strive for peace with everyone,** and for the holiness without which no one will see the Lord. See to it that no one fails to obtain the grace of God; that **no "root of bitterness" springs up and causes trouble,** and by it many become defiled. (Hebrews 12:14–15)

The Blessing of Forgiveness

Is it possible your unforgiveness is robbing you of the joy and peace of Jesus?

> So Jesus said to the Jews who had believed him, "If you abide in my word, you are truly my disciples, and you will know the truth, and **the truth will set you free.**" They answered him, "We are offspring of Abraham and have never been enslaved to anyone. How is it that you say, 'You will become free'?" Jesus answered them, "Truly, truly, I say to you, everyone who practices sin is a slave to sin. The slave does not remain in the house forever; the son remains forever. **So if the Son sets you free, you will be free indeed.**" (John 8:31–36)

Jesus' heartfelt desire is for you to have the full measure of his joy flowing through you. He longs for you to experience an abundance of his presence. But consistently experiencing the fullness of the blessing of the abiding, Spirit-filled life is conditioned upon repenting of the sin of unforgiveness.

Think of the relief it will be to let go of your grudge toward THAT PERSON. You'll be freed up in your mind and your heart to fully enjoy resting in the presence of your friend, Jesus. Think of the contentment you will have, knowing you have been obedient and are no longer bound by the grip of unforgiveness. Rather than repeatedly replaying the offense in your mind, you will be free to embrace this peaceful, life-changing, biblical thinking. Think of the peace you will experience when you choose love over bitterness.

While Jesus was on the cross being crucified despite being sinless, he looked on the men crucifying him and said, "Father, forgive them, for they do not know what they are doing" (Luke 23:34 NIV). The same power and grace that Jesus had to forgive them (and to forgive us), he will give you to help you forgive your offender. Why settle for a few drops of God's blessing and mercy when you are promised an outpouring of God's blessing if you're obedient to forgive?

Personal Story of Forgiveness

> "And when you stand praying, if you hold anything against anyone, **forgive him**, so that your father in heaven may **forgive you** your sins." (Mark 11:25 NIV)

For years I'd had trouble fully forgiving a particular group of people. I would forgive, take it back, forgive, take it back. I was very bitter toward THOSE PEOPLE who did THOSE THINGS to me.

When it came time to write this chapter on forgiveness, I couldn't find the right words. Each repeated attempt was fruitless. Juli and I had a vacation coming up, and I concluded I was tired and a week away would refresh me. When we returned home, I was indeed refreshed, but I still couldn't write about forgiveness.

One morning, while praying with a group of guys, one of them prayed a heartfelt prayer, asking God to bless the same group of people I'd had trouble forgiving. I found myself unable to agree with him in prayer. There was no "amen" in my heart for this group. But as my friend prayed, the Holy Spirit began to convict me of my bitterness toward them. He showed me how I was choosing to let the hurtful actions of a handful of people years ago warp my attitude toward the entire group today.

Over the next week, I asked the Holy Spirit to search my heart and move me past this issue. The Spirit clearly revealed that, while the actions of a few people were wrong, my reaction of unforgiveness was sin, and I needed to repent. I confessed my sin to God, repented of it, and asked him to forgive me. As the burden of my sin of unforgiveness was lifted, I knew I had been set free!

With this freedom from unforgiveness, I found my contempt for THOSE PEOPLE was replaced by compassion. It became easy for me to pray for them. What I had tried so hard to do in my own strength, God freed me to do once I acknowledged my sin and was set free.

While I know my fleshly tendencies may cause me to "take it back" again at some point in the future, it has been quite some time since I forgave them, and I can joyfully and enthusiastically pray for this entire group—including the offending few—for whom God has given me a surprising new appreciation!

Don't Wait to Forgive

I carried that unforgiveness around unnecessarily for years! How long have you been carrying around yours? How many hours, days, or even years have you wasted agonizing over your initial hurt and bitterness toward THAT PERSON or THOSE PEOPLE? Aren't you tired of lugging your unforgiveness with you everywhere you go?

Imagine how much more God would do through your life if you were released from those thoughts and filled with his peace and the power of the Holy Spirit instead. Again, it may require you going to a pastor or counselor for guidance and help, meeting with the other person, perhaps apologizing and asking for forgiveness for your actions, or other steps. But whatever steps are needed, don't wait.

All the promises of blessings of Level III living will be yours when you forgive. Don't wait another minute to get started. Go to Jesus now and ask him to give you the strength to forgive. Jesus will accompany and guide you through it, and it will change your life in ways you never imagined.

Dear friend, my hope for you is that you will experience freedom from unforgiveness as expressed in the apostle Paul's words to the believers in the Corinthian church:

> Even if I caused you sorrow by my letter, I do not regret it. Though I did regret it—I see that my letter hurt you, but only for a little while—yet now I am happy, not because you were made sorry, but because your sorrow led you to repentance. For you became sorrowful as God intended and so were not harmed in any way by us. Godly sorrow brings repentance that leads to salvation and leaves no regret, but worldly sorrow brings death. See what this godly sorrow has produced in you: what earnestness, what eagerness to clear yourselves, what indignation, what alarm, what longing, what concern, what readiness to see justice done. At every point

you have proved yourselves to be innocent in this matter. So even though I wrote to you, it was neither on account of the one who did the wrong nor on account of the injured party, but rather that before God you could see for yourselves how devoted to us you are. By all this we are encouraged. (2 Corinthians 7:8–13 NIV)

ABIDING TRUTH

Because God is holy,
to experience the fullest blessings of the abiding, Spirit-filled life,
forgive THAT PERSON who did THAT THING to you.

REFLECTION QUESTIONS

1. How is forgiving different than forgetting? In what ways are these ideas related? In what ways is there more to it than forgiving and forgetting?

2. Jesus forgave you. Every sin you've committed in your life until now and will commit until you go to be with him is wiped away. What does this mean for how we're all meant to live our lives?

3. Read Matthew 18:23–35. How does Jesus say God will view those who expect forgiveness from him but are not willing to grant it to others? How does this message help you better understand what it means to rest in Jesus' forgiveness?

4. Almost everyone has at one time struggled with unforgiveness. Consider what it feels like. How might you describe what it looks like to live with unforgiveness?

5. Who do you need to forgive? This is a challenging action to take, and it requires Jesus moving in you and through you. *But you can do it!* Pray now and ask for his help. Keep praying for his help until he has sufficiently prepared you to forgive and thereby abide more fully in him.

SONG SUGGESTIONS

"Losing" by Tenth Avenue North
"Forgiveness" by Matthew West
"Broken Vessels (Amazing Grace)" by Hillsong Worship

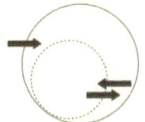

Part Six

HOPE FOR THE WORLD

CHAPTER 16

Faith

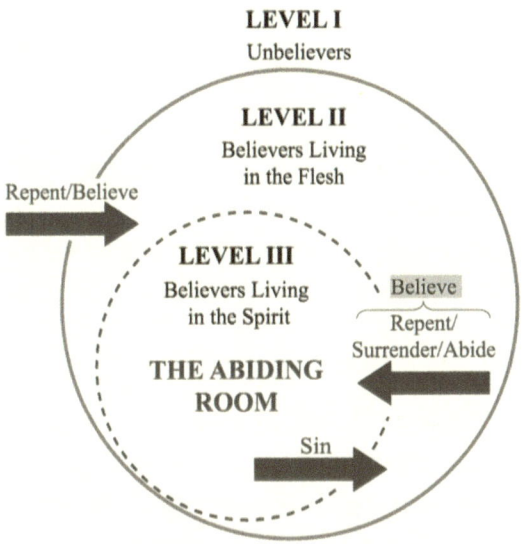

> He [Jesus] was chosen before the creation of the world, but was revealed in these last times for your sake. Through him you believe in God, who raised him from the dead and glorified him, and so your faith and hope are in God. (1 Peter 1:20–21 NIV)

Every aspect of the abiding, Spirit-filled life requires faith. This reality is depicted in the Abiding Room diagram above by placing a bracket beneath the shaded word "Believe" that covers the words "Repent/Surrender/Abide." This indicates it takes faith to repent when you sin. It takes faith to surrender your will to God's will. It takes faith to abide in Jesus.

Faith Defined

What is faith? The Bible describes faith this way: "Now faith is the assurance of things hoped for, the conviction of things not seen" (Hebrews 11:1). And the Merriam-Webster dictionary defines faith as "allegiance to duty or a person."

Faith is our personal choice to believe something or someone is trustworthy. We might also simply say faith is trusting in and following your friend Jesus.

The Bible is the Word of God. It gives testimony to the life, death, and resurrection of Jesus. It gives evidence to the historical work of God in the lives of others in the past, as well as God's instructions and promises to us for today and the future. It takes faith to trust God's Word and act obediently to its instructions for your life.

The Holy Spirit has been given to us to teach and guide us. It takes practice to recognize his promptings, and faith to trust and obey them.

Your Life with Christ Began by Faith

As a follower of Jesus, you started by faith: "For by grace you have been **saved through faith**. And this is not your own doing; it is the gift of God, not a result of works, so that no one may boast" (Ephesians 2:8–9).

You received salvation by faith when you first repented of your sin and received Jesus as Savior. Did Jesus appear to you in bodily form and explain everything to you? No. But by faith you knew he lived, died for your sins, and rose from the dead so you could be forgiven. You didn't understand everything about your sin and God's forgiveness, but by faith, you began following Jesus. Since that time, you've been following Jesus by faith.

Faith Activates the Power of the Holy Spirit

Your faith is essential to experiencing the abiding, Spirit-filled life. The power of the indwelling Holy Spirit is always available to you. But as mentioned in chapter 5, that power must be activated by your faith. Faith is the exciting decision point of trusting God is directing your life and is ready to include you in his work. When you sense God directing you as you read his Word or receive the Holy Spirit's prompting, your next step should be to obey by faith.

Faith is not a chore but an amazing privilege and blessing. You have a God who is great, almighty, sovereign, and infinite, yet so personal that he invites you to trust him and join him in the work he is doing here on earth.

Obedience *to* God means living by faith *in* God. In John 15:10, Jesus said, "If you keep my commandments, you will abide in my love." The way we abide and keep abiding is by obeying God. Faithful obedience continues the abiding, Spirit-filled life and its blessings.

By Faith We Trust God for the Results

We've laid out the benefits of the abiding, Spirit-filled life—love, joy, peace, and all the rest of the fruit of the Spirit. We've said that as we abide in Jesus, we are being filled with the Holy Spirit (The Great 2 for 1) and will bear much fruit. We've said God has even promised us eternal rewards if we take this less-traveled, Spirit-led path.

But how can you know for sure the cost of giving up these things will be worth the benefits you receive? For instance, how can you forgive when the results are unknown? How can you know for sure God will keep his end of the bargain?

Well, you can't know what will happen, but, *by faith,* you can take God at his Word and trust him to be faithful to his promises. Faith is the component that activates every aspect of the abiding, Spirit-filled life. You must trust God whenever you choose to repent, surrender, and abide—leaving the results to him.

If that sounds like a lot to ask—to give up what seems like a lot without knowing exactly what you'll get in return—well, you're right. It is a lot to ask. Nearly everyone feels that way when the time comes to make these life-changing choices to trust God.

Think of it as a heavenly exchange rate. You give up a few earthly pennies and God gives you buckets of heavenly treasure of the abiding, Spirit-filled life in exchange! The exchange rate isn't posted in definite terms. God simply says "Trust me. Trust me for who I am and what I will do."

If all the costs and blessings were known in advance, trusting God wouldn't require faith. You have to give up something with a somewhat unknown cost and trust God for the results (and the timing of those results), which are unknown. That is the essence of faith.

God requires faithful obedience to him, not only to bring about his intended result, but to shape you into the person he wants you to be. As you trust God and see him at work, you are getting to know him better. You are becoming more like Jesus in the process of faithful obedience to God's instructions.

Hopefully, the promises of the abiding, Spirit-filled life laid out in the previous chapters make it apparent that the faith required is well worth the blessing of fully experiencing God in your life.

Faith is a Challenge for Everyone

Faith is something everyone struggles with to some extent. It might help you to know even two of the heroes of the faith struggled with trusting God—Moses and Billy Graham.

Moses, whom God used to part the Red Sea and lead the Israelites out of Egypt, struggled with faith early in his life. When God gave him his first assignment, God told Moses to go to Pharaoh as his messenger and tell Pharaoh what he was going to do. But Moses was afraid and responded, "Oh, my Lord, please send someone else" (Exodus 4:13). Moses' first reaction was fearful reluctance. But when he obeyed, God used him in mighty ways.

A much more recent example is Billy Graham, whom God used to share the gospel of Jesus with people all around the world. Early in his ministry, Billy also struggled with his faith. Before he was a household name, he wrestled with knowing whether he could trust the teachings of the Bible. Here are his words from his autobiography: "I was trying to be on the level with God, but something remained unspoken. At last the Holy Spirit freed me to say it. 'Father, I am going to accept this as Thy Word—by *faith!* I'm going to allow faith to go beyond my intellectual questions and doubts, and I will believe this to be Your inspired Word.'"[1]

As you consider some of the things you sense God is directing you to do right now, it's likely you, too, are feeling fearful, incapable, or unworthy. Be encouraged these feelings are common to everyone—even Moses and Billy Graham.

Starting With One Step of Faith

You'll recall how crossing the Jordan River is symbolic of our crossing from living in the flesh to living in the Spirit. The smaller, innermost circle in the Abiding Room diagram represents the Jordan River. When the Israelites crossed the Jordan River, which was at flood stage, into the Holy Land, it began with a step of faith.

> So when the people set out from their tents to pass over the Jordan with the priests bearing the ark of the covenant before the people, and as soon as those bearing the ark had come as far as the Jordan, and the feet of the priests bearing the ark were dipped in the brink of the water (now the Jordan overflows all its banks throughout the time of harvest), the waters coming down from above stood and rose up in a heap very far away, at Adam, the city that is beside Zarethan, and those flowing down toward the Sea of the Arabah, the Salt Sea, were completely cut off. And the people passed over opposite Jericho. Now the priests bearing the ark of the covenant of the Lord stood firmly on dry ground in the midst of the Jordan, and all Israel was passing over on dry ground until all the nation finished passing over the Jordan. (Joshua 3:14–17)

God could have easily stopped the flow of the Jordan River without any action on the part of the Israelites. Why did he require them to first step into the water? Because God requires faith on the part of his followers.

It had to be frightening for the Israelites to step into the rushing waters of the Jordan River. It would have been much easier to stay in the desert where they were already comfortable with their surroundings.

God uses the story of the Israelites as they crossed over from the desert to the Holy Land to illustrate how he requires faith from us. We must trust him as we take a step out of our comfort zones and enter into his abiding presence.

Only a Mustard Seed of Faith

Jesus says you need only a mustard seed of faith: "If you have faith like a grain of mustard seed, you will say to this mountain, 'Move from here to there,' and it will move, and nothing will be impossible for you" (Matthew 17:20).

In his mustard seed lesson, Jesus makes the point you need faith, but you don't need *great* faith. A mustard seed is one to two millimeters (that's less than half the size of a BB for a BB gun). If you have even a speck of faith, God can use that little granule of faith to do what is impossible for you to do in your own strength and strategies. God can use your speck of faith to move a mountain no one thinks can be moved.

As you've been reading about the abiding, Spirit-filled life, what do you find yourself desiring? More intimacy with God? Overcoming a bad habit or addiction? A restored relationship? Hope in the midst of circumstances that may never change?

As mentioned earlier, in the first few years of our marriage, I was harsh and critical toward Juli. I wouldn't listen to anyone. When she shares her story, Juli describes those years of our marriage this way: "In our home, there were two ways of doing things—Kevin's way and the wrong way."

Juli would tell me how my actions were hurting her, but I didn't care. She had tried patient, thoughtful reasoning in addition to our marriage counseling, but nothing changed—at least not for long. Throughout those years, Juli maintained the belief that God *could* change me, but she began wondering whether God *would* change me. God's kindness is *meant* to lead each of us to repentance, but *would* I repent if God opened my eyes to my sin?

None of our friends or family knew what was going on in our marriage. That was because (1) I didn't behave this way toward Juli or anyone else in public, and (2) Juli didn't complain about me to anyone. Despite my antagonistic behavior toward her in private, I can't recall Juli being anything but respectful toward me in public. She was consistently obedient to Ephesians 5:33 which says, "Let the wife see that she respects her husband."

How did she do it? By trusting God to do what she knew she could not. Juli is an abider. She was living by the power of the Holy Spirit. The Holy Spirit was filling her with the love, joy, peace, patience, kindness, goodness, faithfulness, gentleness, and self-control she needed to not only cope with me but to respect me in spite of my fleshly actions.

And her faith gave her the hope described in Romans 5:

> And we boast in the **hope** of the glory of God. Not only so, but we also glory in our sufferings, because we know that suffering produces perseverance; perseverance, character; and character, **hope.** And **hope does not put us to shame, because God's love** has been poured out into **our hearts through the Holy Spirit,** who has been given to us. (Romans 5:2–5 NIV)

While Juli continued to pray for me to change, her faith gave her the perseverance, character, and hope that sustained her. Though I showed no sign of changing, with her remaining mustard seed of faith she persisted in asking God to change me into a gentler husband. And in his timing, God chose to sovereignly move the mountain of my pride. By his grace and for his glory, he intervened, I repented, and he changed my defiant heart. To this day we can't fully explain it, but we are immensely grateful for God's faithfulness.

When I look back on what Juli did and how God blessed us through her faithful perseverance, I think of these words in Galatians, "And let us not grow weary of doing good, for in due season we will reap, if we do not give up" (Galatians 6:9).

Faith Brings Hope

Let's close this chapter by looking at a few encouraging reminders from the Bible, telling us who God is and what he promises.

God loves you with an infinite love. He cares about what you are experiencing.

> Cast all your anxiety on him because he cares for you. (1 Peter 5:7 NIV)

> "Though the mountains be shaken and the hills be removed, yet my unfailing love for you will not be shaken nor my covenant of peace be removed," says the Lord, who has compassion on you. (Isaiah 54:10 NIV)

God is sovereign and able to do whatever he chooses.

> "For nothing will be impossible with God." (Luke 1:37)

God keeps his promises.

> "Know therefore that the Lord your God is God; he is the faithful God, keeping his covenant of love to a thousand generations of those who love him and keep his commandments." (Deuteronomy 7:9 NIV)

God blesses you when you trust him.

> Blessed is the man who makes the Lord his trust. (Psalm 40:4)

> For the Lord God is a sun and shield; the Lord bestows favor and honor; no good thing does he withhold from those whose walk is blameless. Lord Almighty, blessed is the one who trusts in you. (Psalm 84:11–12 NIV)

> Delight in the Lord, and he will give you the desires of your heart. (Psalm 37:4)

> And without faith it is impossible to please him, for whoever would draw near to God must believe that he exists and that he rewards those who seek him. (Hebrews 11:6)

You can have hope in the plans God has for you.

… that you may know what is the hope to which he has called you. (Ephesians 1:18)

"For I know the plans I have for you," declares the Lord, "plans to prosper you and not to harm you, plans to give you hope and a future." (Jeremiah 29:11 NIV)

Dear friend, persevere in your faith. Faith will activate the Holy Spirit's power within you to both guide and sustain you. God is producing godly character and hope in you as you trust him, and he will do great things through your small acts of faithful obedience!

ABIDING TRUTH

To experience the fullest blessings of the Spirit-filled life, have faith that Jesus can live his life in and through you.

REFLECTION QUESTIONS

1. A common definition of faith is "believing in things you cannot see." You put your faith in these types of things every day—the coffee machine that makes your morning beverage, the car that starts and takes you to work, your job that continues to carry on, your health you take for granted or are working hard to improve. How is your spiritual faith different from faith in these everyday situations? What happens when your faith fails?

2. Putting our faith in Jesus when we abide is the activating factor for his using us in the lives of others. What's one example of when you had faith and he used you for better things? What made that situation unique for you or the other people involved?

3. In this chapter we read, "Obedience *to* God means living by faith *in* God." Think of a personal situation where you saw someone exhibit great faith. What did that look like? What are you facing today that requires you to have faith? Where might Jesus be asking you to abide more fully and step out in faith, trusting he will guide you?

SONG SUGGESTIONS

"What Faith Can Do" by Kutless
"Faith" by Jordan Feliz
"I Will Fear No More" by The Afters

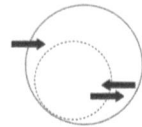

CHAPTER 17

Church Unity and Revival

"I do not ask for these only, but also for those who will believe in me through their word, that they may all be one, just as you, Father, are in me, and I in you, that they also may be in us, so that the world may believe that you have sent me. The glory that you have given me I have given to them, that they may be one even as we are one, I in them and you in me, that they may become perfectly one, so that the world may know that you sent me and loved them even as you loved me." (John 17:20–23)

This chapter consists of two parts—Church Unity and Revival. Church unity arises naturally within a body of believers when they are practicing Jesus' presence and living the abiding, Spirit-filled life. Revival is a special and dramatic movement of God's Spirit within God's people that then flows outward to others.

CHURCH UNITY

The Spirit-Filled Church

On his last night before going to the cross, Jesus prayed for you! The overriding heart of his prayer was unity within the church. Why did Jesus use his last moments before being arrested to pray we would be one? For our own comfortable lives? No. As shown in the passage above, he prayed for unity, "so that **the world may know** that you sent me and loved them even as you loved me."

The four verses of Jesus' prayer in John 17 at the start of this chapter are essentially two sets of verses that repeat the same theme. Jesus prays two things would become reality: (1) we would be one, and (2) so the world may believe God the Father sent him. Jesus' prayer emphasizes his hope for the church to live in unity so we can show a lost but watching world that God loves them. What a magnificent blessing that God allows us to impact the world through our obedience to him!

When we're living Level III lives in the Abiding Room, we're living in harmony not only with God but with each other. Remember the chocolate milk video? When the world encounters Spirit-filled people, it's a sweet experience. The world notices when our chocolate milk is stirred up and we're living the loving and joyful lives God intends for us.

Up to this point, we have examined many challenging topics with respect to our personal lives. We've seen the many personal blessings that result from obedience. Now we'll see the blessing that arises from a similar obedience of a local church, as well as God's people collectively throughout the world.

The Harmonious Early Church

Jesus' prayer in John 17 for those who *would* believe came to fruition quickly. A little less than two months later, at Pentecost, for the first time, all God's children were indwelt and filled with God himself in the person of the Holy Spirit. The church was born and was immediately healthy, vibrant, and impactful!

Let's revisit how the Bible describes the new church in Acts:

> And they devoted themselves to the apostles' teaching and the fellowship, to the breaking of bread and the prayers. And awe came upon every soul, and many wonders and signs were being done through the apostles. And all who believed **were together and had all things in common.** And they were selling their possessions and belongings and distributing the proceeds to all, as any had need. And day by day, **attending the temple together and breaking bread in their homes,** they received their food with **glad**

and generous hearts, praising God and having favor with all the people. And the Lord added to their number day by day those who were being saved. (Acts 2:42–47)

Now the full number of those who believed **were of one heart and soul,** and no one said that any of the things that belonged to him was his own, but **they had everything in common.** And with great power the apostles were giving their testimony to the resurrection of the Lord Jesus, and great grace was upon them all. **There was not a needy person among them,** for as many as were owners of lands or houses sold them and brought the proceeds of what was sold and laid it at the apostles' feet, and it was distributed to each as any had need. (Acts 4: 32–35)

These were believers rejoicing in their salvation and praising God. Their love for God and each other was contagious in their communities. The early church illustrates for us today that, in a healthy church, we are to spend time together, enjoying each other's company (not in isolation) and impacting our communities as a result.

The World is Watching

"In the same way, let your light shine before others, so that they may see your good works and give glory to your Father who is in heaven." (Matthew 5:16)

Perhaps one of the few things we can agree on today is there are a lot of disagreements in the world. And the church is not exempt from differences of opinion related to worldly issues, nor to our own unique disagreements. There will always be disagreements over many topics, but within the church these disagreements do not need to result in division.

In times of societal turmoil, must the church be caught up in the fray? Or is it possible that turbulent times create the greatest opportunity for the church to stand out as an oasis of love and peace? The biblical call to the church and to the individual is the same—to be the united, Spirit-filled Body of Christ. This is what Jesus prayed for us to be.

The apostle Peter expressed it this way:

> **Finally, all of you, have unity** of mind, sympathy, brotherly love, a tender heart, and a humble mind. Do not repay evil for evil or reviling for reviling, but on the contrary, bless, for to this you were called, that you may obtain a blessing. (1 Peter 3:8–9)

When we begin to access the power of the Holy Spirit, we unleash the dormant power of the church. The unlimited potential of changing the world is inside every follower of Jesus. The only question is whether it's being fully utilized. When you're letting the life of Jesus flow through you, your individual life is a ministry that bears much fruit to the people in your sphere. To an even greater extent, a community of Spirit-filled believers in a local church is a powerful weapon to pierce the darkness of a lost world and bring many to salvation:

> Put on then, as God's chosen ones, holy and beloved, compassionate hearts, kindness, humility, meekness, and patience, bearing with one another and, if one has a complaint against another, forgiving each other; as the Lord has forgiven you, so you also must forgive. And above all these put on love, which binds **everything together in perfect harmony**. And let the peace of Christ rule in your hearts, to which indeed **you were called in one body**. And be thankful. (Colossians 3:12–15)

Think of the possibilities if we were to allow God to open our eyes fully to Spirit-empowered living. We would no longer look to institutions powered by the mere strength of men to resolve the problems of society; we would instead look to a Spirit-empowered church. The Great Provision of the Holy Spirit and Spirit-filled living can resolve not only many of the problems of today but carry out the Great Commission of Jesus to make disciples of all nations as well.

Local churches living Spirit-empowered lives are God's instruments for carrying out his plan for a lost world. What an amazing thing it will be to see churches overflowing with Spirit-filled people having everything in common and fulfilling our God-given assignments!

REVIVAL

Rediscovering the Holy Spirit

While I am by no means an expert on revival, the accounts of revival in the Bible and subsequent history give us vivid stories of what revival is and how it arises.

Revival refers to moments in time when God's Spirit moves within his people to bring them into full contact with him, his truth, and his power. There are points in time when God chooses to orchestrate a special movement and revive the hearts of the people within his church. The word "revival" applies whether the movement impacts a small region (such as a city or town) or spreads to a larger region (such as an entire country).

Revival takes place when God's Holy Spirit moves powerfully among believers, bringing deep conviction of sin and widespread confession and repentance. Fleshly believers who've been unattuned to the Holy Spirit suddenly encounter him and become Spirit-filled believers empowered by him. Many believers move from Level II to Level III living.

Many unbelievers who were far from God become new followers of Jesus. As we'll soon see, revival may result in joyful singing and praising God for hours, spontaneous worship continuing throughout the night for many days, stolen goods being returned to vendors, and underreported taxes being paid to the government.

In times of revival, discouragement, dissatisfaction, and desperation are replaced by a renewed hope for the future. Broken relationships are restored. Love between people is reestablished and made evident. Men and women's vertical relationships with God and horizontal relationships with each other are revitalized. In short, wrong things are made right.

Doesn't that sound like something we need today?

Biblical Revival

As we saw in Acts 2, the church was born through revival within the Israelites' community. Everyone who repented and put their faith in Jesus for the forgiveness of sins received the indwelling Holy Spirit. This revival created a noticeable difference that caused people to choose between accepting or rejecting Jesus. In subsequent days, many were added to the church, and many opposed the church.

Examples of Revivals in America

Trying to catalog the exact place and time revival starts, as well as the number of people saved when it occurs, is impossible. Nevertheless, there have been times in America and throughout the world when there was no debate that significant spiritual revival was sweeping through communities and even nations. There is no question our hope for revival lies in our reliance upon the person of the Holy Spirit, who is the source of all revivals.

Let's look at three revivals in American history to see how they impacted America.

The Great Awakening

The 1730s and 1740s are remembered as a time of great preaching by George Whitefield and Jonathan Edwards. This revival changed American culture as hundreds of new churches were formed to accommodate the remarkable growth.

God called many young men into ministry as pastors. Colonies found greater unity through their shared faith, which helped prepare them for the American Revolution. Though it is often forgotten as being the source, the Great Awakening still has remnants of its impact on American society today.

Prayer Revival of 1857–1858

In 1857, Jeremiah Lanphier, a quiet businessman who had been appointed as a missionary in New York City, was a significant instrument of God in revival. Lanphier posted flyers around the city, inviting anyone to join him to pray once a week at noon at his church.

The first week, six men showed up. Within two weeks, forty were praying and decided to begin praying daily. Soon, many churches were filled with people praying, and many were being saved. Secular newspapers regularly reported on the prayer meetings. Eventually, there were noon prayer meetings in over 10,000 cities and towns in America. Ultimately, more than one million people gave their lives to Jesus.

Asbury Revival of 1970

On February 3, 1970, revival occurred at Asbury College (now Asbury University) in Kentucky when the Holy Spirit moved on campus. For more than a week, worship and praise continued at the chapel on campus throughout the day and night. Relationships within the student body and between students and faculty were healed. Many students went from lukewarm faith to a passionate zeal for God. The news accounts drew people from other states to come to the campus to see for themselves, and they, too, were impacted by the Holy Spirit.

But it didn't stop at the campus. Many Asbury students traveled to their hometowns as well as to churches around the country to share their stories. Frequently, those trips led to similar impact in towns and churches. The Holy Spirit used their stories to impact hearts, and many relationships were restored. Churches where worship had grown stale came alive with great joy as they encountered God.

One of the unique aspects of the Asbury revival is that the initial days of its occurrence were reported by local news reporters and can be viewed online today. I encourage you to look at the video titled "The Story of the 1970 Asbury Revival" on abidingroom.com. It includes views of the revival as it happened on campus. Imagine if something like that happened at your college campus, church, or community, and how those stories and pictures could spread even more rapidly today through online and social media accounts!

You Can Be a Part of the Coming Revival

> "**If my people** who are called by my name humble themselves, and pray and seek my face and turn from their wicked ways, then I will

hear from heaven and will forgive their sin and heal their land." (2 Chronicles 7:14)

A. T. Pierson was a nineteenth-century pastor and advocate of missions who was determined to see the world evangelized in his generation. He is widely credited as saying, "There has never been a spiritual awakening in any country or locality that did not begin in united prayer."

While there is a great deal of wonderful mystery about revivals, and it is impossible to predict when God will orchestrate such a movement, the Bible is instructive as to his conditions for revival. Prayer precedes revival, and revived people pray in the Spirit. Through prayer, our will becomes aligned with God's will. Revival begins within *some* of us, which leads to prayer from *more* of us, which meets God's conditions to send his Holy Spirit to move through *all* of us.

Revival is not a spectator sport. God calls you and me, as his people, to participate in ushering it in. The catalyst for such a mighty move of God is prayer. While spiritual movements are mysterious in their timing, magnitude, and length, there's no denying that, when they are later analyzed, it's discovered they began with prayer.

It is clear from 2 Chronicles 7:14 God has given us instructions as to what we are to do if we desire to see him bring revival: (1) humble ourselves, (2) pray for revival, (3) seek God's face, and (4) turn from our wicked ways.

Doesn't God's prerequisites for revival on a larger scale sound quite a bit like his conditions for revival on a personal basis? Whether revival is personal or across a group of people, the biblical pattern for revival is the same—if we, God's people, will be humble, pray, seek his face, and repent, he will heal us spiritually.

Spirit-filled people pray Spirit-led prayers that can touch the heart of God and set in motion movements beyond our greatest expectations. God made this conditional promise to "my people" (the church). This verse also tells us the healing of entire nations begins with God's people getting into a right relationship with him.

Jesus says the right relationship is the abiding relationship, and the abiding relationship leads to answered prayer: **"If** you abide in me, and my words abide in you, **ask whatever you wish,** and **it will be done for you"** (John 15:7). Here are two more promises from Jesus for answered prayer regarding many things, including revival:

> "Truly, I say to you, whatever you bind on earth shall be bound in heaven, and whatever you loose on earth shall be loosed in heaven. Again I say to you, if two of you agree on earth about anything they ask, it will be done for them by my Father in heaven. For where two or three are gathered in my name, there am I among them." (Matthew 18:18–20)

> "Whatever you ask in my name, this I will do, that the Father may be glorified in the Son. If you ask me anything in my name, I will do it." (John 14:13–14)

Did you notice each of the passages above includes the word "if"? *If* we abide and ask, God will answer. He will answer when and how he chooses—frequently not when or how we expect—but he nevertheless promises to answer.

Are we willing to pay the price in order to experience revival in our day? The need is apparent and enormous, and God is able and willing to move in mighty ways if we meet his conditional promise to pray.

All of this begs the questions: Are you ready to begin asking? Are you ready to ask God to bring a spiritual movement into your life? A spiritual movement in your church? A spiritual movement in your community? A spiritual movement in your nation? What an amazing privilege God has given you to be a part of bringing about something so significant and dramatic as revival!

Since 2003, a small group of friends and I have gathered together once a week in the early morning to pray for revival. We have sensed God is preparing his people for another mighty movement of his Spirit that will heal our land. We're greatly encouraged as we continue to learn of many others who are praying for and believing the same thing. Many are praying and believing God's love, mercy, and compassion are going to bring about another significant revival.

The news of the refining fire of revival in even one location could be easily communicated throughout the world through today's technology, so anyone in the world could be impacted.

Many are hoping for Jesus to return and remove them from the mess of this fallen world. But what will Jesus find if he returns today? What spiritual condition will he find us in? Will he find a church that is spiritually alive or one that is spiritually napping? How exciting it is to petition Jesus for revival, so, when he returns, he will find the church on fire for him!

As an abiding, Spirit-filled follower of Jesus, you have the potential to be an instrument God uses to bring change to a hurting world. God has promised he will move in mighty ways when he is asked. Will you take him up on his promise and be part of the coming revival?

> Now to him who is able to do immeasurably more than all we ask or imagine, according to his power that is at work within us, to him be glory in the church and in Christ Jesus throughout all generations, for ever and ever! Amen. (Ephesians 3:20–21 NIV)

ABIDING TRUTH

Local churches where people are living Spirit-empowered lives are God's instruments for carrying out his plans to reach a lost world.

REFLECTION QUESTIONS

1. When you think of the word "revival," what comes to mind? Think of a time when you experienced something resembling a revival of your faith. Take a moment to reflect on what that was like. What might you be able to repeat from that process to keep your faith fresh?

2. Think about the last time you were part of a church-related activity where God worked through you to bless others. What about that experience makes it something you would want to repeat?

3. Church unity and revival are often spoken of in broad terms, but they can also be aimed at specific areas. Where in your life do you see unity and movement? Where might there be disunity or stagnation? What could you be doing to invite Jesus into those areas and make them flourish in his care?

4. A significant aspect of church unity is being engaged in a local congregation. If you're not yet engaged, now is the time to start. If you're already involved in a local church, how can you be more fully engaged and contribute to the unity and growth of the people in your church?

5. Take a few minutes now to pray for the revival of your church community. Ask Jesus to send his Spirit to fill the hearts and minds of everyone in your congregation. Ask him to show you how to support unity in your groups and abide in him as a living example of faith.

SONG SUGGESTIONS

"God of Revival" by Bethel Music, featuring Brian and Jenn Johnson
"Build Your Kingdom Here" by Rend Collective
"God of This City" by Chris Tomlin

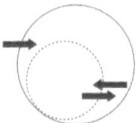

CHAPTER 18

A Call to Action

"I came that they may have life and have it abundantly." (John 10:10)

As we close, give yourself a pat on the back for making it to the end! It would have been easy to quit along the way. But, as we have explored the abiding, Spirit-filled life, hopefully the Holy Spirit has begun a work in you, gripping your heart to relentlessly pursue experiencing him more fully in your life. And if you have already been living the Spirit-filled life, let these lessons encourage you to continue in your present walk.

Next Steps

What should you do now? It is very likely that, throughout these lessons, the Holy Spirit has been prompting you as to what he wants you to do next.

For instance, you may be sensing God is leading you to begin practicing abiding in him by finding ways to intentionally bring Jesus to mind throughout your day. I used to wear a watch that beeped every hour as a reminder to rest in Jesus. I was often surprised to discover where my attitude and thoughts were when that watch beeped!

Maybe God has revealed someone you need to forgive, or an area in your life you need to surrender, or some other action you need to take.

The next steps the Holy Spirit is leading you to take may seem daunting now, but your obedience will give you rest, restoration, and refreshment. And as you are obedient to what the Spirit is prompting you to do, do so with an enthusiastic expectation that God will impact your life and the lives of those around you.

Further Study

You may sense God is directing you to delve further into some particular area of your spiritual life. Appendix 2 has a list of books you may wish to read for additional direction. These books were selected for their quality and applicability to each topic.

On the abidingroom.com website you'll also find a bookmark you can print out. This tool combines the main diagram with the primary points of this book. I believe you'll find the bookmark helpful to refer back to as a brief overview of the book.

15 Minutes a Day That Will Change Your Life

God is always available and ready to guide you. He's always eager to hear your cries and prayers. Let me suggest that, for each of the next 30 days, you choose a specific time and place to spend at least 15 minutes daily with God. In addition to anything else God is already prompting you to do, pray the two prayers below each day with a sincere desire for God to answer them.

Prayer 1

Lord, let me see me the way you see me.

Prayer 2

"Search me, God,
and know my heart;
test me and know my anxious thoughts.
See if there is any offensive way in me,
and lead me in the way everlasting."
(Psalm 139: 23–24 NIV)

These are the prayers I prayed daily for a very short period in 1999 that led to my spiritual breakthrough. When I first started to pray these two prayers, I asked Juli what she thought I would discover. Speaking with her typical gentleness, she said she thought I would discover God loved me more than I knew. I said I thought I would discover some sin in my life that needed to be dealt with. We were both right. God brought about wonderful changes in our lives.

These are prayers God will answer! What a blessing it is to hear from God and know he cares deeply for you. Be still and listen. When God speaks, don't hesitate. Obey!

Take Obedient Action Now

Trust God and know he will reward you for obedience in taking the next steps. He's planned a life of meaning, purpose, and power for you. Jesus is walking right next to you to help you, and the indwelling Holy Spirit will guide and empower you in every step of your journey of obedience.

Though we are ordinary people, we are indwelt by an extraordinary God. God has called and equipped ordinary people like us for extraordinary purposes.

Be Encouraged!

In conclusion, be encouraged to know:

> As you *repent* of known sin (Mark 1:15),
> *believe* Jesus can live his life in and through you (Galatians 2:20),
> *surrender* your will to the Father (Romans 12:1–2),
> *abide* in the Son (John 15:5), and are thus
> *filled* with the Holy Spirit (Ephesians 5:18),
> God will give you the desires of your heart (Psalm 37:4), and
> do more through your life than you asked or imagined
> (Ephesians 3:20).

May our heavenly Father continually remind you of his unwavering love for you. May he grant you immense grace in your pursuit of him. May he reveal to you in ever-increasing magnitude his plan for your life. May the Holy Spirit fill you to overflowing. And may you experience Jesus' profound love for you as you rest in him and experience his abiding friendship.

ABIDING TRUTH

To experience the abiding, Spirit-filled life,
your next steps are
to be obedient to the Spirit's leading
and establish healthy spiritual habits.

REFLECTION QUESTIONS

1. What's one thing you've learned from this study that has changed your view of the Holy Spirit?

2. How will the information you've encountered here help you to practice a closer walk with Jesus? What does that look like?

3. If you had to describe your experience in studying this material to someone, what would you say?

4. If the Holy Spirit has identified something you need to be paying attention to now, don't wait! Abide fully in him and pray he will lead you to whatever actions need to be taken to bring his urgings to life in you and through you.

SONG SUGGESTIONS

"Do It Again" by Elevation Worship
"Brave" by Nichole Nordeman
"Live Like That" by Sidewalk Prophets
"All of Creation" by Mercy Me

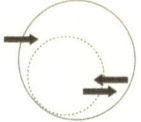

APPENDIX 1

The Good News

Take a moment to consider where you currently stand with God.

Are you living in harmony with God or separated from him?

As is explained in chapter 1, because of sin, Adam and Eve were separated from God.

The Bible says all people are sinful. As we saw with Adam and Eve, because God is holy, sin separates us from God.

> All have sinned and fall short of the glory of God. (Romans 3:23)

> The wages of sin is death. (Romans 6:23)

God sent his Son, Jesus, to pay the penalty for our sin, and make a way for us to cross over from eternal separation from God to eternal life with God.

> "For God so loved the world, that he gave his only Son, that whoever believes in him should not perish but have eternal life." (John 3:16)

> "To all who did receive him, to those who believed in his name, he gave the right to become children of God." (John 1:12)

Jesus said if you reject him in this life, he will reject you in the next life. But, if you receive him as Savior in this life, he will welcome you into his family forever—now in this life and forever in the next life in heaven.

"Everyone who acknowledges me before men, I also acknowledge before my Father who is in heaven, but whoever denies me before men, I will also deny before my Father who is in heaven." (Matthew 10:32–33)

"Whoever believes and is baptized will be saved, but whoever does not believe will be condemned." (Mark 16:16)

Do you have eternal life with God?

Jesus said eternal life is a gift from God, but it must be received. The wonderful news is that once it is received, it is permanent.

"I give them eternal life, and they will never perish, and no one will snatch them out of my hand. My Father, who has given them to me, is greater than all, and no one is able to snatch them out of the Father's hand." (John 10:28–29)

Becoming a follower of Jesus is putting your faith in his death on the cross for your sins and his resurrection from death for your eternal life.

Pray to receive eternal life with God.

If this expresses the desire of your heart, pray this prayer to receive eternal life today:

Dear Lord Jesus, thank you that you paid the full penalty for all of my sins, and rose from the dead to give me eternal life. By faith, I receive you as my Savior and desire you to be Lord of my life.

If you prayed this prayer, you are now a child of God! You have received the Holy Spirit who will be your guide and teacher. Your first steps should include beginning to read the Bible daily and finding a Bible-believing church to attend regularly.

Welcome to God's family!

APPENDIX 2

Recommended Reading List

Chapter 1: The 3 Levels of Life in the Old Testament

"The Levels of Life" by Dr. Charles Stanley, https://www.intouch.org/watch/sermons/levels-of-faith-in-the-life-of-the-believer

Chapter 2: The 3 Levels of Life in the New Testament

"Have You Made the Wonderful Discovery of the Spirit Filled Life?" by Dr. Bill Bright, https://www.cru.org/us/en/train-and-grow/spiritual-growth/the-spirit-filled-life.html

Chapter 6: Be Filled with the Spirit

Experiencing the Holy Spirit by Andrew Murray

Chapter 8: The Vine and the Branches

The True Vine by Andrew Murray

Chapter 9: The Abiding Friendship

Practicing His Presence by Brother Lawrence & Frank Laubach

Chapter 10: Surrender Your Will

Absolute Surrender by Andrew Murray

Chapter 11: Surrender Your Self-Effort

They Found the Secret by V. Raymond Edman

Chapter 12: Surrender Your Worldliness

The Treasure Principle: Unlocking the Secrets of Joyful Giving by Randy Alcorn

The Man in the Mirror by Patrick M. Morley

Chapter 13: God Is Holy

The Pursuit of Holiness by Jerry Bridges

Chapter 14: Repentance

Every Man's Battle: Winning the War on Sexual Temptation One Victory at a Time by Stephen Arterburn and Fred Stoeker

Every Woman's Battle: Discovering God's Plan for Sexual and Emotional Fulfillment by Shannon Ethridge

Chapter 15: Forgiveness

Total Forgiveness by R.T. Kendall

Chapter 17: Church Unity and Revival

Revival Fire by Dr. Wesley Duewel

One Divine Moment: The Account of the Asbury Revival of 1970 edited by Robert E. Coleman, *25th Anniversary Edition* edited by David J. Gyertson

APPENDIX 3

Compilation of Abiding Truths

Chapter 1: The 3 Levels of Life in the Old Testament

> The Old Testament establishes and illustrates The 3 Levels of Life.

Chapter 2: The 3 Levels of Life in the New Testament

> The New Testament confirms and illustrates The 3 Levels of Life.

Chapter 3: The Battle of the Spirit and the Flesh

> An internal battle between the indwelling Holy Spirit and your flesh goes on every minute of every day, but you can consistently win the daily fight as you choose to walk in the Spirit.

Chapter 4: Experiencing the Holy Spirit's Joy and Peace

> When you walk in the Spirit, you will experience love, joy, and peace.

Chapter 5: The Power of the Holy Spirit

> As a follower of Jesus, you are indwelt by the Holy Spirit. He gives you the power to carry out God's commands and live a life of freedom from sin.

Chapter 6: Be Filled with the Spirit

> As a follower of Jesus, you are always indwelt with the Spirit.
> And as you are obedient, you will be filled with the Spirit.

Chapter 7: The Great 2 for 1

> The Great 2 for 1:
> As you abide in Jesus,
> you are being filled with the Holy Spirit.

Chapter 8: The Vine and the Branches

> When you abide in Jesus,
> you will bear much fruit.

Chapter 9: The Abiding Friendship

> Jesus calls you friend
> and enjoys spending time with you.

Chapter 10: Surrender Your Will

> To experience the fullest blessings of the Spirit-filled life,
> surrender your will to God's will.

Chapter 11: Surrender Your Self-Effort

> To experience the fullest blessings of the Spirit-filled life,
> surrender your self-effort and rest in Jesus.

Chapter 12: Surrender Your Worldliness

> To experience the fullest blessings of the Spirit-filled life,
> surrender your worldliness.

Chapter 13: God Is Holy

> Jesus has made a way for you to enter
> into the presence of the Holy God
> by making your body the temple of his Holy Spirit.

Chapter 14: Repentance

Because God is holy
to experience the fullest blessings of the Spirit-filled life,
repent of all known sin.

Chapter 15: Forgiveness

Because God is holy,
to experience the fullest blessings of the abiding, Spirit-filled life,
forgive THAT PERSON who did THAT THING to you.

Chapter 16: Faith

To experience the fullest blessings of the Spirit-filled life,
have faith that Jesus can live his life in and through you.

Chapter 17: Church Unity and Revival

Local churches where people are living Spirit-empowered lives
are God's instruments for carrying out his plans
to reach a lost world.

Chapter 18: A Call to Action

To experience the abiding, Spirit-filled life,
your next steps are
to be obedient to the Spirit's leading
and establish healthy spiritual habits.

APPENDIX 4

Compilation of Suggested Songs

Chapter 1: The 3 Levels of Life in the Old Testament

"Egypt" by Bethel Music, featuring Cory Asbury
"No Longer Slaves" by Bethel Music, featuring Jonathan David and Melissa Helser
"Perfectly Loved" by Rachael Lampa, featuring TobyMac

Chapter 2: The 3 Levels of Life in the New Testament

"The Struggle" by Tenth Avenue North
"Let It Fade" by Jeremy Camp
"All You Got" by DC Talk

Chapter 3: The Battle of the Spirit and the Flesh

"Battle Belongs" by Phil Wickham
"Disappear" by Out of the Grey
"Death Was Arrested" by North Point Worship

Chapter 4: Experiencing the Holy Spirit's Joy and Peace

"Peace Be Still" by The Belonging Co
"Safe" by Phil Wickham

Chapter 5: The Power of the Holy Spirit

"Same Power" by Jeremy Camp
"Whom Shall I Fear [The God of Angel Armies]" by Chris Tomlin
"God of Wonders" by Mac Powell, with Cliff and Danielle Young

Chapter 6: Be Filled with the Spirit

"Fullness" by Elevation Worship

"Presence (My Heart's Desire)" by Newsboys

Chapter 7: The Great 2 for 1

"In This Room" by We Are Compass Worship

"By Your Side" by Tenth Avenue North

Chapter 8: The Vine and the Branches

"New Wine" by Hillsong Worship

"Abide With Me" by The Worship Initiative, featuring Bethany Barnard and John Marc Kohl

"Tend" by Bethel Music, and Emmy Rose

Chapter 9: The Abiding Friendship

"I Am" by Jill Philips

"Christ In Me" by Jeremy Camp

"Just Give Me Jesus" by Unspoken

Chapter 10: Surrender Your Will

"Control" by Tenth Avenue North

"Make Room" by The Church Will Sing/Community Music

"I Surrender All" by Jadon Lavik

Chapter 11: Surrender Your Self-Effort

"Dear God" by Cory Asbury

"Just Be Held" by Casting Crowns

"Truth Be Told" by Matthew West

Chapter 12: Surrender Your Worldliness

"I Surrender All" by Clay Crosse

"Have It All" by Brian Johnson

"The Motions" by Matthew West

Compilation of Suggested Songs

Chapter 13: God Is Holy

"Holy Forever" by Chris Tomlin
"Revelation Song" by Phillips, Craig and Dean
"Ancient Gates" by Brooke Fraser Ligertwood
"Temple" by Brandon Lake

Chapter 14: Repentance

"As You Find Me" by Hillsong United
"Point to You" by We Are Messengers
"Holy" by Nichole Nordeman

Chapter 15: Forgiveness

"Losing" by Tenth Avenue North
"Forgiveness" by Matthew West
"Broken Vessels (Amazing Grace)" by Hillsong Worship

Chapter 16: Faith

"What Faith Can Do" by Kutless
"Faith" by Jordan Feliz
"I Will Fear No More" by The Afters

Chapter 17: Church Unity and Revival

"God of Revival" by Bethel Music, featuring Brian and Jenn Johnson
"Build Your Kingdom Here" by Rend Collective
"God of This City" by Chris Tomlin

Chapter 18: A Call to Action

"Do It Again" by Elevation Worship
"Brave" by Nichole Nordeman
"Live Like That" by Sidewalk Prophets
"All of Creation" by Mercy Me

The QR Codes below contain a playlist of all the songs recommended.

Playlist Using Apple Music

Playlist Using Spotify

APPENDIX 5

Suggested 12–Week Group Schedule

WEEK 1 Welcome to *The Abiding Room*
Chapter 1: The 3 Levels of Life in the Old Testament
Chapter 2: The 3 Levels of Life in the New Testament

WEEK 2 Chapter 3: The Battle of the Spirit and the Flesh
Chapter 4: Experiencing the Holy Spirit's Joy and Peace

WEEK 3 Chapter 5: The Power of the Holy Spirit
Chapter 6: Be Filled with the Spirit

WEEK 4 Chapter 7: The Great 2 for 1
Chapter 8: The Vine and the Branches

WEEK 5 Chapter 9: The Abiding Friendship

WEEK 6 Chapter 10: Surrender Your Will
Chapter 11: Surrender Your Self-Effort

WEEK 7 Chapter 12: Surrender Your Worldliness

WEEK 8 Chapter 13: God Is Holy

WEEK 9 Chapter 14: Repentance

WEEK 10 Chapter 15: Forgiveness

WEEK 11 Chapter 16: Faith

WEEK 12 Chapter 17: Church Unity and Revival
Chapter 18: A Call to Action

Notes

Chapter 7: The Great 2 for 1

1. Billy Graham, *The Holy Spirit: Activating God's Power in Your Life* (Nashville, TN: W Publishing Group, 1988), 242.

Chapter 11: Surrender Your Self-Effort

1. Walter Hooper, editor, *The Collected Letters of C.S. Lewis, Vol, III, Narnia, Cambridge and Joy, 1950–1963* (San Francisco: HarperSanFrancisco, 2007) 111, emphasis added.

Chapter 13: God Is Holy

1. A.W. Tozer, *The Knowledge of the Holy* (New York: HarperCollins, 1961), 105–6.

Chapter 14: Repentance

1. Richard Owen Roberts, *Repentance, The First Word of the Gospel* (Wheaton, IL: Crossway Books, 2002), 209.

Chapter 16: Faith

1. Billy Graham, *Just as I Am: The Autobiography of Billy Graham* (Grand Rapids, MI: HarperCollins Worldwide, 1997), 139, emphasis in original.

About the Author

Since 2002 Kevin has taught classes about the wonderful truths of the abiding, Spirit-filled life. During that time, he has enjoyed meeting one-on-one with young men, teaching them to live similarly. Kevin retired in 2023 after 40 years as a financial advisor. He and his wife, Juli, grew up and still reside in the Phoenix area. They have three grown children.